Praise for K

What a story! Andy Dietz had me captivated with his story of being kidnapped in Hungary, facing death against impossible odds, and discovering a powerful desire to live. He challenged and inspired me to live that way every day, with a passionate, desperate desire—not just to live, but to experience life to the fullest. You will be blessed!

NEAL JEFFREY, ASSOCIATE PASTOR,
PRESTONWOOD BAPTIST CHURCH, PLANO, TX;
FORMER ALL-AMERICAN QUARTERBACK FOR BAYLOR UNIVERSITY, AND
SAN DIEGO CHARGER; AUTHOR OF *IF I CAN, Y-Y-YOU CAN!*

One of the ways we remind ourselves and each other of God's faithfulness is the telling of stories. This story is not only full of danger and excitement; it also reminds us of a God who is in control.

MICHAEL KELLEY, EXECUTIVE EDITOR OF HOMELIFE MAGAZINE;
DIRECTOR OF DISCIPLESHIP AT LIFEWAY CHRISTIAN RESOURCES

An overseas mission experience turned into a nightmare for Andy Dietz. *Kidnapped in Budapest* is an emotional and gripping account of that experience, but beyond the panic and intrigue that ensued, it is a challenge to put life values into perspective. Desperation reaches a new dimension when one's life is on the line, but with eternity in view one should be ever desperate to know God.

JERRY RANKIN, PRESIDENT EMERITUS OF
INTERNATIONAL MISSION BOARD, SBC

There may be no greater need in the modern Western church than up-to-date eyewitness accounts of God's presence, power, provision, and protection. Andy Dietz reminds us we still serve the Great I Am, not the great "I Was." My faith was stirred; my courage and confidence were emboldened. And I was reminded that *'He will be with us…even unto the ends of the Earth.'*

Great read; great reminder.

MIKE CURRY, PRESIDENT AND FOUNDER OF
LIGHT MINISTRIES, INC. CONWAY, AR

Kidnapped in Budapest

the chilling, true story of a missionary...

KIDNAPPED IN BUDAPEST

ANDY DIETZ

Deep River
BOOKS

Kidnapped in Budapest
The Chilling True Story of a Missionary
Copyright © 2014 by Andy Dietz

www.andydietz.net
kidnapped98@gmail.com

This book is published in association with The Benchmark Group
Literary Agency, Nashville, TN, benchmarkgroup1@aol.com.

Unless otherwise noted, Scripture taken from the NEW AMER-
ICAN STANDARD BIBLE®, Copyright © 1960, 1962, 1963,
1968, 1971, 1972, 1973, 1975, 1977, 1995 by The Lockman
Foundation. Used by permission.

Scripture marked "KJV" is taken from the King James Version
of the Holy Bible, public domain.

Deep River Books
Sisters, Oregon
www.deepriverbooks.com

ISBN – 13: 9781940269122
ISBN – 10: 1940269121

Library of Congress: 2014936275

Printed in the USA

Cover design by David Litwin, Pure Fusion Media

DEDICATION

Never in my wildest dreams did I think I would ever be kidnapped, nor did I ever expect my life to be threatened. Even with all the assistance from home, it still came down to me alone, to escape the situation. In reality, we may never know how God worked everything out through the prayers and extraordinary actions of faithful people.

Between seventy and one hundred people gathered at my house and at the church to pray. Others, thanks to the Internet and phone calls, were praying around the world. Michael and Jodina Plumley made their Western Union account available, buying me some time, and State Senator Larry Combest engaged the FBI and the Budapest police on my behalf. Some of the first to arrive at my home to pray and make phone calls were: Leon Mitchell, one of our local attorneys and a church elder; Pastor Gregg Simmons; and Les Sharp. These and many others were a great support to my wife as the ordeal unfolded.

However, the most incredible response came from my wife, Becky, who remained calm as far as I could detect in every conversation we had, and prayed with the passion that I've seen from her on so many occasions before. Honestly, as I experienced the love of my family and community, I was given the encouragement and hope I needed to fight on.

It's often in challenging times that the Church shines the best, and the true hearts of its people are exposed. That was true in my case, but it was not the first or last time that God's people responded so tremendously.

This book is dedicated to everyone involved, named or unnamed, who prayed and acted on my behalf to secure my freedom. To God be the glory in all things!

CONTENTS

INTRODUCTION

In the summer of 1998 I was kidnapped and held for ransom by the Hungarian Mafia in Budapest, Hungary. I remember the date well because it was the same day that two of our African embassies were attacked by terrorist organizations in Kenya and Tanzania. Unfortunately, the embassy attacks only complicated the struggle of an already intense nightmare.

No one ever expects something like the events of that day to happen, but when they do, the emotions are far too great to describe. They poured in like an unexpected landslide and grew most intense only after the event itself had long passed. As I began putting the details of my kidnapping down in print, it stirred, to a lesser extent, the emotions once again.

Looking back, I know that the entire event was orchestrated to serve a greater plan in my life. Sometimes we are searching for more—a greater purpose, a reason to be—but it takes something drastic to awaken us to the awareness of our need. We know something is wrong. We know we need a new direction or focus, but we hunker down inside, needing a push, or in my case a *shove,* just to encounter God in such a way as to finally hear! Leading up until that day, it was as though He was *screaming* at me, and I was walking around with ear buds in my ears, oblivious to His summoning voice.

From the outside, no one would have known anything was wrong. My life was exciting compared to most, but I had come to the place where everyone arrives sooner or later, a place where faith does not seem like enough. My blessings were many at the time. I had four awesome kids who were seeking God's direction in their lives. My wife, Becky, could not be a more giving and selfless mate or a more perfect mother to my children. I had just transitioned from student minister to pastor of missions and evangelism because of the growing interest of my home church in reaching the world. I was doing exactly what I felt called by God to do. Missions gave me the opportunity to continue my connection with students and fulfill the Great Commission at the same time, taking the gospel into all the world.

So what was wrong? What glaring need was I ignoring? Simply put, I had a desperate need to know God more. Things, people, even family, nothing and no one can supply what only God can fill! We stack more and more activities and programs into our lives, endeavoring to be fulfilled, but instead we wear ourselves out trying to do what only God can do. It is the same process that drug addicts and alcoholics follow, only the drug addicts and alcoholics are filling their lives with bad things, and we "normal" people are filling our lives with superficially good things. But God does not want us to do more. He wants more of us so that what we do will be done in His Spirit and by His power!

On that day in Hungary, God changed my world. He put me in a place where I had to listen. Whether I obeyed or not was up to me, but I had to listen! I'm not saying that if you share my need to know God more that there's an encounter with the Hungarian Mafia in your future—God's first choice for us is to "be still and know that I am God" (Psalm 46:10, KJV). He would much prefer to gently guide us along to His plan and purpose, just as we would prefer to lovingly guide our children in the right path. But realistically, no one guides their children along to adulthood without some amount of firm correction taking place along the way. That's what God did for me in Hungary. Because of this experience, my entire perspective on *life* has changed! This life is not about us, it is about God. Since it is about God, our focus should be on Him. I don't just live life anymore, I *experience* life!

The Bible addresses believers in Christ as priests. In a recent study of the tabernacle by Zach Neese, entitled *How to Worship a King,* I was reminded that priests are to "carry the presence of God." We are essentially ambassadors of God. Every person we meet, every situation we are in, every encounter we face should inspire us to represent God. When we do this, life takes on an entirely different dimension.

I make a concerted effort to encourage other people to experience life in God, but I'm more or less convinced that it takes something drastic in most of our lives to ever bring us to that place. It seems to me that most people are just happy with the status quo. They just live life: go to school, find a mate, get a job, have a family, and maybe go to church. It's a sad thing that it took such a major wake-up call in my "living life" to see that life was meant to be experienced!

My hope, as you read, is that you will experience this story with me. I hope you will begin, as I did, to understand how to experience life and not just live it. Those who just live life seldom change lives. Those who experience life often see lives changed.

My life verse is John 14:6: "Jesus said to him, 'I am the way, and the truth, and the life; no one comes to the Father but through Me.'" In this passage, Thomas asked Jesus a question. He asked the right person, he got the right answer, and he made the right decision. Until my kidnapping, I had asked the right question…to the right person…but made the wrong decisions. I just continued to live life my way, and never really heard and followed God's plan.

When faced with death, a desperation to live kicks in. May we all be as desperate to know God as we are to live.

"That He would grant you, according to the riches of His glory, to be strengthened with power through His Spirit in the inner

man, so that Christ may dwell in your hearts through faith; and that you, being rooted and grounded in love, may be able to comprehend with all the saints what is the breadth and length and height and depth, and to know the love of Christ which surpasses knowledge, that you may be filled up to all the fullness of God.

"Now to Him who is able to do far more abundantly beyond all that we ask or think, according to the power that works within us, to Him be the glory in the church and in Christ Jesus to all generations forever and ever. Amen."

EPHESIANS 3:16–21

CHAPTER 1

Facing Death

I was standing at an outdoor sidewalk bank pressed in by several of the Mafia thugs, waiting for my card to be declined once again, when the bad news came. As the teller refused the card, the "suit guy" standing to my left slammed his fist to the counter, screaming Hungarian at me. I asked the interpreter what he said, and she told me, "Now you die!"

Who knew that going into a restaurant to eat would escalate into being kidnapped and held for extortion? That it would lead to possible death? During our orientation to Budapest just five years earlier, my missions team had been told that there was a Mafia element in some of the local establishments and that we needed to always be aware of our surroundings and any unusual activities taking place around us. But no one ever imagines being in a life-ending situation, especially Americans, who typically live in Small Town USA and encounter little greater than an occasional fender bender.

No one really wants to die, but when that probability arrives, a person will do whatever it takes to live. In that moment I felt overwhelming fear, helplessness, and panic, but I remember experiencing desperation far above all the other emotions. I was alone in a strange country, surrounded by people I didn't know or choose to be with, who were extorting money from me and had just told me I was going to die! This was really happening to *me!*

That day was my first time to actually think about my own death. Oh, I had considered the thought that I would die someday, I think everyone does, but to essentially be told that my death was imminent was a totally different experience. I instantly turned myself to escape mode but continually thought about death, and how it would feel, and the method they would use. I was John Wayne on the outside but felt like Pee-Wee Herman on the inside.

It was not the first time I had been around death, and every time had left a mark. My twin brother, Phil, and I traveled and sang from our high school years until seven years after our graduation from college, and we saw many things transpire during that time.

One day while driving through central Texas from an engagement on a hot July day, I began moving to the left lane of a four-lane highway to allow a motorcyclist to enter from the on-ramp. As I was changing lanes, the motorcycle grazed the rear bumper of an eighteen-wheeler ahead of him, which flipped the cycle. I had to swerve just to miss the man's head as it opened up on the hot Texas pavement in front of me. As eyewitnesses to the accident, we had to remain until the police released us from the scene. Our mortality became even more real to us as we experienced just how vulnerable human life was.

On another occasion, during the time we sang with the Royalheirs gospel quartet, we pulled up to a small country Methodist church for a Sunday morning concert. I remember it being a cold and windy February morning. Only the church and a modest four-room white house across the road occupied the corner of the country intersection, surrounded by dormant dry wheat fields. I was the first person out of the van, and I heard a desperate female voice screaming at me, "Help my baby! Help my baby!" I turned to look and saw a woman coming from the house across the road, barefoot and dressed only in a short, revealing white nightgown.

At seven o'clock in the morning I wasn't exactly thinking very clearly, but I found myself following this woman as she dragged me by the hand to her little four-room house. I must admit, I thought I was being set up. She pointed me to a dark bedroom on the right, just as I saw a man out of the corner of my eye putting on his Levi's in the bedroom to my left. I thought, *Why did she not awaken this man to deal with the problem instead of dragging me into the situation?*

I continued on into the bedroom and saw an infant baby, cold, blue, and lifeless, lying in the crib. There was no pulse or breath at all, so it was obvious the baby had been dead for a couple of hours. I turned to hug the crying mother and tell her that her baby was gone. I walked into the kitchen while the man explained that the baby had cried most of the night. "Do ya want a beer?" he said as he finished zipping up his jeans.

"No, but may I use your phone?" I asked. Then I called the sheriff, who arrived at the house within a few minutes. I made a lot of assumptions that day but never heard any further report about the incident. Events like this began shaping the realities of life in my mind after a fairly simple and uneventful childhood. I saw that life was not always easy or kind to people outside my protected world. These events motivated me to reach the lost world with the hope of Christ.

One of the most horrific experiences my brother and I had was following a special concert at a church we had sung in several times. The concert was on a Sunday evening prior to the renovation of the church sanctuary, which would begin the following morning. Work had already started on the choir loft and baptistery area, leaving the interior wall and ceiling studs exposed. The church was full, the people were excited, and they wanted to give us a love offering to show their appreciation. We were spending the night with one of the church families following the concert, so the pastor asked if we would come by the church the next morning to pick up the offering. The pastor came by the family's house that evening after the concert. He asked the family if Phil and I could go out with him for a few minutes, but the host explained that his wife had just cooked supper and it was ready to eat. He was invited to join us, but he excused himself and left.

We arrived at 7:30 the next morning, only to find the church buzzing with police and law enforcement officers. To our shock, we walked in and discovered that the pastor had been found hanging in the baptistery.

We will never know what he wanted to talk about the night before, but I've always wondered if it would have made a difference. The police asked us to leave, and we never heard much more about the incident, but we were asked to sing at the funeral a few days later. I remember my brother and me driving away hardly saying a word for hours, just praying for his wife and young family as we traveled to our next engagement. Later, as we verbalized our feelings, we wondered what could bring a person to this decision. Suicide has always been a mystery to me; no matter how down or depressed I've been, it was never an option. I've wondered many times what secrets or feelings could be great enough for anyone to consider this choice. I was especially puzzled that a pastor would make such a decision. I found myself wondering if the hope of the gospel was really enough in such a terrible and dark world. Again, this event just drove me further to want to help, to find answers, and to bring solutions to hurting people in a more tangible way.

Fast-forward about thirty-five years to the summer of 2012. I received a phone call from a young lady who had tracked me down. She lived in Albuquerque and had made a business call to my older brother's church. When she heard his name, she inquired if he was related to or knew The Dietz Brothers. He of course did, and he gave her my number to call. She asked me if I remembered singing in that Texas town about thirty years earlier.

"Yes! I remember it well," I replied.

"Well," she said, "that was my dad that hung himself." Tears began to fill my eyes as she continued. "There was a song you sang at the funeral that helped me make it through that terrible tragedy...'I've Been to Calvary.' I just wanted to tell you thank you!" I believe she was about ten at the time of her dad's death.

These events were all very emotional and moving experiences for my brother and me, and in Hungary, their memory only made death even more real as I faced it myself. I remember wondering how I would respond if I were a family member of any of the people who went through these situations. All of these things made death real to me. As a young twenty-something at the time, death was not a common thought in my life; most people my age felt virtually invincible. The experiences certainly gave me illustration and motivation to encourage other young people who might be without Christ and possessed the same conviction of invincibility to consider Christ, because no one knows the day or hour of their appointment with Him.

Facing death also gave me urgency to move from a traveling ministry to a local and more personal ministry where I felt I could make a greater impact on young lives by investing more time in relationships. In the traveling ministry we saw God accomplish much, and we met friends for life who were fellow servants in a similar work—evangelists, celebrities, and musicians who would eventually partner with us in future projects. To this day I will occasionally meet someone who attributes their walk with Christ to the Dietz Brothers or Royalheirs ministry. But I meet far more who were in our student and missions ministries in local churches who will point to those ministries as life-changing for them. While traveling ministry was fruitful, God was encouraging me to help change young people's lives through a more personal and relationship-oriented method. The deaths we experienced gave me an urgency to invest more quality time than traveling ministry gave us to spend with students.

In fact, it was the pastor's suicide in Texas that clinched that desire for a change in me. And I wasn't alone. My brother and I had planned, unknown to one another, to talk about personal ministry change during a California road trip. As I introduced the subject while driving our bus down the road, I saw a quizzical smile on Phil's face as he said, "I was just debating how to bring this subject up to you, too!"

Though I didn't know it then, the change we made, in part because of that pastor's death, would eventually lead me to face my own death in Budapest—and more than that, to face my desperate need to learn to experience life to a new degree in God. That day was still far away, and I couldn't have imagined it then. But the road was laid out, and I was beginning to walk it.

CHAPTER 2
Ministry Changes

Not long after the death of the pastor, I transitioned from traveling concert ministry into student ministry. It had been a desire of my heart to do so for a while, as I saw more and more young people making poor decisions. During my college years, I made some very poor choices as well, which motivated me to help teenagers avoid the same mistakes.

I remember Bill McKinney, a star football player at the college I attended, who later played linebacker for the Chicago Bears. Bill was instrumental in discipling me through my difficult times, which eventually encouraged me to do the same for others. Bill and his wife, Carol, helped lead the West Texas State University Campus Crusade for Christ ministry and influenced me more than they may ever know. Not many people knew at the time the difficulties I was going through, but the unconditional love I felt from Bill and Carol helped to turn my life around.

Following my senior year at WTSU, I met Becky on a blind date arranged by my roommate's girlfriend. I had dated several girls during my college days and met some very nice people; it was just that I had not met the *right* one. I was taking a several months' hiatus away from dating and was not thrilled about the blind date Donna had arranged, but when I met Becky, it was love at first sight. I remember a shapely, ninety-eight-pound gorgeous redhead walking into the dorm lobby while I was only hoping this was my date. But what I remember most is her beaming smile and contagious laugh. She knew who I was from my traveling days, but we had never met before the date.

We were married about a year later. Becky was a Pampa girl—the rival school to Borger—so I really received a lot of grief from my Borger friends until they got to know her. Then that all changed. Becky had two brothers, a younger sister, and great parents. Her family was very accepting of me, and we became very close in a relatively short time. It wasn't long after the wedding that we decided to start a family, and three of our four children (Matthew, Amy, and David) were born while we were still living in Amarillo. Zach came along after we moved to Oklahoma.

I began my student ministry at Second Baptist Church, a great little fellowship in Amarillo, Texas. The church had a small group of about twenty or thirty students and some of the most giving and humble people I've ever served. For Becky and me, as a young couple, it was a perfect church to develop good friendships and cut our teeth on student ministry. Phil took a student ministry position at Skelly Drive Baptist Church in Tulsa shortly after I went to Second Baptist, and I remember meeting several of his disciples—like Troy and Tim, who eventually went into the ministry themselves. It all confirmed that our decision to move from traveling to local ministry was the correct choice.

Becky was busy with kids during our early years but still found time to host couples in our home and build really close relationships with those our age. I remember playing Rail Baron, a board game, during parties at our house every other weekend in Amarillo. The men would play the game, and the ladies would visit and corral kids until the wee hours of the morning. I discovered during those weekends how gifted Becky was at relationships and hospitality. She continues using her gifts in ministry and still finds herself busy speaking, discipling, and teaching. Her best and favorite gift of all is that of unconditional love, which she lavishes on our ten amazing grandchildren. Much of our ministry style was learned and developed in Amarillo and with the wonderful people of our church.

It was very hard to leave Second Baptist, but after four years we were asked to take a large ministry of four hundred students in Broken Arrow, Oklahoma, a bedroom community of Tulsa. It was in Broken Arrow that my ministry blossomed, and I learned much about vision and organization. The student music program was led by a willing layman, and I watched it struggle at fifteen or so youth, so I approached the interim music minister about restructuring the church's student music program with a team approach. Our idea was to train the students in voice, drama, sound, lighting, instruments, and public speaking. We scheduled mission projects once a quarter and encouraged the students to use their talents during the projects.

The student music program grew from fifteen to almost three hundred in just one year. Rosy Greer, a former Los Angeles Ram NFL football player, was so impressed with the students that he offered his time to come encourage them. My confidence grew, and with it an understanding of God's true calling and a passion for His will. The student ministry grew to over six hundred during my four years there, but an offer to move back to my hometown of Borger, Texas, interested me because it was a smaller community in which to raise my family.

Borger is where missions became a larger part of my student ministry. The church had a genuine heart for missions; they gave financially, prayed earnestly, and went occasionally. During my traveling years, my brother and I began to identify personalities of the different churches we encountered. Some were very giving, others very evangelistic, and others strong in Bible teaching and discipleship. The church in Borger had a definite passion for missions, so I began to involve our students in more mission projects to align with the heart of the church and to help inspire their own walk with God.

My personal heart for missions began during a tour with the United Service Organization (USO), which provides programs and live entertainment to United States troops. This was following my senior year in college, and it was when I saw, for the first time, the poverty of Panama and Cuba—people literally living in huts made of nothing more than cardboard and plastic sheeting. The first book I ever read was *Bill Wallace of China,* which I checked out from the church library as an elementary student. The book gave me my first exposure to missions and revealed how hard and dangerous missions could be—and yet exciting too. Looking back, that book probably gave me a heart for the people of China, for whom I would later pour fifteen years of my life in traveling and ministering there. Becky and I have "our girls," ten young ladies in China whom we've sponsored, led to Christ, and discipled since they were twelve years old. They have now finished college, some have married, and two have babies whom Becky and I were privileged to name. They are all involved in the underground church and have developed into godly young believers and soul winners.

Although I developed a heart for missions, I think my desire to tell people about Jesus was greater. And yes, there is a difference! The very first person I led to Christ was in Fort Worth, Texas, during the Explo '72 conference at the Cotton Bowl in Dallas, Texas. We went out in teams of two, one guy and one girl, in the Metroplex area, knocking on doors and sharing the Four Spiritual Laws. During my training, Bill Bright himself led me through the Four Laws—with me not knowing that he had written *The Four Laws* and was founder of Campus Crusade for Christ!

The very first door my partner and I knocked on was that

of an Hispanic lady who was obviously upset and crying. To our surprise, she invited us in. I asked her, in my limited Spanish, if she was okay and if we could help, but she turned the conversation to inquiring why we were there. Not knowing what else to do, I began sharing my salvation testimony and the Four Spiritual Laws. The lady readily accepted Christ and began telling us that the reason she was crying was that her husband had just left her the night before. During her story, she reached under the couch and retrieved a gun, telling us that she was just about to kill her two-year-old son and herself at the moment we knocked on the door!

That one event impacted my life forever, discovering how important it is to share Christ and to hear from God! Later we learned that the lady led her husband to the Lord using the same Four Spiritual Laws, and that their marriage and family were being restored. Because of these events, a desire was birthed in me to share the love of Christ at home and around the world.

One of the most rewarding mission projects I led was to an orphanage in Reynosa, Mexico. We took about sixty students and adults each spring break and taught VBS, changed diapers, cooked meals, washed clothes, repaired buildings and vehicles, provided dental work, and just loved on the kids. In the beginning of the work, the orphanage had about thirty kids, ages birth to sixteen. They had three cinder-block buildings, all with just dirt floors, with no windows or doors, just openings. Rampant flies attached themselves to the children like leeches. When our ministry came to an end, we had built or remodeled two dorms, a guys' and girls', both with showers; built a kitchen and dining hall; and repaired a building that became the orphanage's chapel.

The ministry in Reynosa taught me how important it is for students to experience missions for themselves. The result was a *transfer* of the parents' faith to the students. This principle is *life changing!* Until a person's faith becomes his own, it is dead faith. This is the tragedy of the traditional church: our students are searching for God, but we want them to find Him through *our* method of worship and *our* traditional ways of expressing Him. Once again, it becomes all about us! If we had scriptural ground on which to stand, it would be a different debate. But our typical complaints are loud and noisy praise music, standing too long, or the way students dress. It's the same argument in almost every church I visit. If I am not mistaken, the Word tells us to "make a joyful noise unto the Lord" (Psalm 100:1, KJV)! To "praise Him with loud cymbals" (Psalm 150:5)! To "enter His gate with thanksgiving, and His courts with praise" (Psalm 100:4a)! God also tell us that "Man looks at the outward appearance, but the LORD looks at the heart" (1 Samuel 16:7b).

This final verse condemns many of us, because even *Jesus* would not be welcome in countless congregations according to our standards of dress. My philosophy is "Come as you are, and let God transform you into what you will be." It is not our job to change lives; it is God's! We are only to be priests, carrying the presence of God, experiencing life as we follow the Way, the Truth, and the Life.

Working at the orphanage in Reynosa was the best process we had to let students see God for themselves, and for each one to develop his or her own faith and walk with God. We worked with the orphanage for eleven years and built some lifelong relationships. I remember, in particular, a three-year-old boy named Jacabo, who had big brown eyes and a smile a mile wide. He became one of the teams' favorite kids. Five years after we ended our work with the orphanage, I was asked to travel back to Reynosa to help a local church with a project. I flew to McAllen, Texas, and drove across the border to the church. I was to meet the pastor and his wife at their house that afternoon. When I arrived at their home, I walked in and greeted the pastor and his wife, and then the pastor wanted to introduce me to his adopted teenage son. As I reached out to shake the young man's hand, he said, "You don't have to introduce me to Andy...I'm Jacabo from the orphanage!"

What a pleasant surprise! The pastor went on to inform me that Jacabo was now nineteen and studying to be a pastor. We all sat down as Jacabo began to explain to the three of us how my church's ministry in the orphanage had helped change his life. He told us that many churches would come to the orphanage each year to teach VBS or just help out a little. They would work during the day and then go back across the border at night. Not many of the churches would ever come back the following years, so few relationships were ever built.

Then he said, "But you guys came back year after year. You changed our diapers, put us to bed, and washed our clothes. We knew that you loved us."

While I was wiping the tears from my eyes, Jacabo said something I will never forget. "As I watched your people, I decided if that's what real Christians are like, then I want to know their God!" Jacabo told me that it was during one of our many Bible stories at the orphanage that he prayed to receive Christ.

It was stories like Jacabo's that encouraged my call to missions. After ten years in Borger as student pastor, and seeing the ministry grow from eighty students to almost three hundred, I transitioned from student ministry to missions. At that time I began incorporating a drama in many of our mission projects— a drama that would eventually lead to ministry in Europe, and to the day that would change my life.

CHAPTER 3

Mr. President

The missionary journey that began in places like Reynosa would eventually take me and my church teams to Eastern Europe. The church's first visit to Hungary was in 1994, and we continued to go back for the next four years. In the spring of 1998, I made a phone call to a friend, Walker Moore, who produced and owned the drama *Freedom*, which our church had performed in several countries around the world. The drama is a depiction of the life of Christ focused mainly on His death, burial, and resurrection. The story, set in medieval times, uses a gentle ruler and his son and incorporates a sword fight timed to music and narration. It has been produced in several languages, and the drama team simply performs the drama to the music as it is narrated.

During the Dietz Brother days, Phil and I had teamed up with evangelist Michael Gott on many occasions, doing citywide crusades and youth evangelism conferences. Michael is known as the Billy Graham of Russia and was beginning a work in Belarus. He approached me while we were doing ESL ministry in Poland together with the idea of bringing the drama team to Belarus as part of his summer crusades there. But even though I was excited to team up with Michael again, God seemed to have another plan. After several months of the visa process, we were unable to secure the required papers. Ministry continued to be strong in Budapest, with other teams from America adopting projects there, so we wanted to move to the relatively untouched European region of Belarus.

I was very discouraged during the process of trying to obtain the visas and forgot, for a time, that God was still in control and that this was a perfect opportunity for a divine appointment. I've experienced many events in my life which could only be explained by God, but I occasionally seem to forget them.

When Walker Moore answered the phone and I identified myself, his response was, "I can't believe you're calling me!"

"Why?" I asked.

He explained that he had just finished a conversation with the president of Hungary. According to Walker, a Hungarian boy had been following one of the drama teams around Budapest the previous summer, watching the drama and listening to the message. Now that he mentioned it, I remembered a boy, about fourteen or fifteen, meeting us at the subway every day. He would ask us at the end of each night where we would be the following morning. Budapest is a city of over two million people and is divided into twenty-three sectors, so we would travel to a different sector each morning. Every day started at sunrise with devotionals and a breakfast of hard bread, Nutella, and orange juice, and a four-block walk to the nearest subway connection.

At the beginning of the two-week trip, we never even thought to really look for the boy, thinking he was a typical teenager who would sleep his summer mornings away, but without fail, he would always be there waiting. That was during our fourth summer to perform the drama in Hungary, and the boy who had followed us around was apparently the son of the Hungarian president! He had received Christ at what was supposed to be our final presentation in Hungary.

The young boy later shared his experience with his dad, which prompted the phone call to Walker. The president was asking for a team to come back to Budapest and perform the drama even in previously restricted areas of the city. Walker told the president that he didn't know of any teams that would be in Budapest that summer…they were all scheduled to be in other countries. That is why my call was such a surprise! Walker and I had both been part of many divine appointments, so we shouldn't have been amazed at yet another miracle from God.

Walker and I met one another while we were both doing student ministry in Tulsa, Oklahoma. We traveled together to several student conferences, and our wives traveled with us to a Metro Youth Ministers Caribbean cruise and a youth camp in Grindelwald, Switzerland. Walker and I also journeyed to Europe for two weeks just three years after the Berlin Wall fell, looking for the best city to initiate the drama ministry. We wanted this both for the people of Eastern Europe and for the students we would bring with us.

We both felt strongly that students needed a "rite of passage" in their lives. This biblical process was something that moved teenagers into adulthood but was lacking in modern-day American students. The biblical model, to put it simply, took young twelve- or thirteen-year-old boys and had their elders test them rigorously. When they passed, they became men and were then held responsible as adults. The closest event in American culture would be the receiving of a driver's license, but this really involves no responsibility on the teen's part other than passing a simple driving test. However, mission trips gave teens a significant task: taking the gospel of Christ to an unfamiliar culture and language and requiring the teens to be responsible adults. Europe was just beginning to open up to the gospel, and this was a perfect time to research the possibilities for this "rite of passage" type of ministry.

Walker and I took a train from Amsterdam to Prague, then to Budapest and several cities in between. Sometime later, Walker chose Budapest to begin his drama ministry; at the time of my story, it had been running for five or six years.

So, at the invitation of the Hungarian president, I returned with a team of high school students, college students, and adults to Budapest in July of 1998 for our fifth summer of doing the drama at parks, prisons, and bus stops. Sometimes, two or three hundred people, young and old, would gather at the drama sites to watch, many times with mouths wide open and eyes filled with tears as the truth of the drama touched their hearts.

Freedom takes hours of hard work to learn and perform. Everything is timed to the music throughout the entire production, with moving and dramatic music. I have been in, and have seen, the drama hundreds of times, and I still find myself moved each time it's performed. The highlight is a choreographed sword fight timed to intense and dramatic orchestrated music. The sword fight involves eight people slashing and dodging swords (PVC pipe) over their heads and through their legs until the evil knights are defeated. The drama ends with an emotional crucifixion scene, a dramatic resurrection, and the defeat of the evil knight in a final and intense fight to the finish. When done right, it is very powerful and moving. Most crowds find themselves unconsciously standing to their feet as they battle with us to the very end!

I remember one performance where we gathered at a small park surrounded by several twenty-story high-rise apartments, and where kids were playing in the sandboxes below. The locals called it Prostitute Park. A busy street ran by on one side, lined with tall trees and park benches. The park benches had several questionable-looking women seated there beside two men, who I assume "employed" the ladies. Other than an occasional drunk, we had not really encountered any opposition to the drama, but I had warned the team to always be ready for anything. They were trained to continue the drama no matter what, unless otherwise instructed by me.

We set up near one of the sandboxes, and a crowd of children and adults began to gather close. Many of the residents filled the balconies surrounding the park, and we proceeded with the drama. Even the prostitutes and two men eventually turned from their "business" and began to watch the event with intrigue.

Only one or two minutes in, we noticed eggs being thrown at us from one of the balconies above. A team member was hit in the chest but continued on as if nothing had happened.

When team members were not in a scene, they would gather in a back corner and pray in a tight circle we called a "pod." I remember a *big* prayer meeting going on as we all prayed out loud in our pod during that scene! The team continued on as instructed, and the audience began to laugh and jeer.

Within minutes, as the drama moved to the sword fight and then the crucifixion scene, everyone from the balcony, all the children, and even the prostitutes were focused as though the scene was *personally* happening to them. We gave the invitation, and most of the crowd, even the egg throwers, prayed to receive Christ, along with six or eight gang members! I was very proud of our team that day, to say the least.

It was at this point that our team really jelled—not that they weren't close and working as a team before, but for the first time, these young people themselves had experienced a form of persecution. Like Christ, they were heckled. Like Christ, they were rejected and scorned. Their message was being refused. For some, the experience moved them from their parents' faith to their own faith, from living life to experiencing life! *Transfer* happened!

For me, the experience strengthened my faith, but not to the depths that God had planned for me in just a few days. This was not yet the wake-up call that I needed. God had something much deeper for me to experience. I know now that my impending detour through Moscow, and its challenges, would be a gentle way for God to prepare me for a deeper work that was to come. Not only that, but the drama team had, in that moment, just become more effective prayer warriors on my behalf, as we would soon part ways for *my* "deeper work"!

During much of my church ministry, I was given responsibility over benevolence. It taught me to be compassionate without compromise. I learned discernment and how to recognize a lie from truth. I learned quickly that many people became high-maintenance individuals. It was always, "Give me this," "I need that," and "Can you help me with this?" It was never, "How may I help you?" or "How can I return the favor?" I wonder sometimes if God patiently listens to our narcissistic requests hoping we will stop thinking about ourselves long enough just to listen to Him. Living life is about us; *experiencing life* is about God, and learning where and how He is working. Even when we are supposed to be serving Him, it's easy to slip into just living life or doing things solely for our own benefit.

In my life verse, where Jesus declares Himself "the way, the truth, and the life," what stands out to me is the word *life*. The verse is progressive; we begin with Jesus as the *way*, and move through *truth* to get to *life*. When *truth* sets you free, you begin to experience *life*. Until my kidnapping, even though I was serving God, in many ways I just continued to live life my way, and I never really heard and followed God's plan.

Not long after our experience of being jeered and egged during the drama, I would learn what it might feel like to face death for Christ's sake. That experience would forever change my perspective and the way I try to experience life to the fullest.

CHAPTER 4

Moscow

After a very rewarding two weeks of ministry, I sent our fifteen-member team home to Texas and traveled alone from Budapest to Moscow, Russia, to meet James, a former student from our church. He had begun a ministry in Moscow, so our church was sending me to help with several projects and to deliver some money to get the ministry started. James was one of thirteen missionaries from our church in Borger. The church was good about encouraging our own missionaries and would occasionally travel or send a team to their locations to help.

Moscow was in a transition period at the time of my visit. The Berlin Wall had come down just nine years earlier, and most of the government entitlement programs had been discontinued. Those with entrepreneur spirits had jumped on the free enterprise wagon, but the poor and elderly were left to fend for themselves. What the government had once provided—health care, housing, and benefits—was suddenly and unmercifully stripped from the people, and the corrupt and evil element stepped in to seize the moment! To say the least, Moscow was in disarray.

I remember arriving at the dark, dingy Moscow airport only to find no one there to greet me. James and I had no way to communicate and hadn't made any plans other than to meet at the gate. I waited for several minutes, then made my way through security to the arrival hall. Immediately, people began to barrage me with questions that I didn't understand, grabbing me and my bags, trying to force me into their taxis, and relentlessly pursuing me until I escaped into a stinky, nasty, unkept bathroom stall. The men were still buzzing like piranha on the other side of the partition. I had several thousand dollars on my person, which made me more uncomfortable than I would normally have been. After a few minutes, the men finally left the stench of the bathroom to stalk other prey. It looked as though the toilet had not been flushed for several days, so I didn't know how much longer I could stay inside my temporary refuge.

I cautiously ventured back out into the arrival hall to look for James as I tried to avoid the feeding frenzy of the Russian opportunists. I found a corner in which I could stand that was furthest from the gate entries into the arrival hall and out of sight of the taxi stands, yet visible to the entry where I thought James might come in.

After twenty or thirty minutes, we finally connected and drove on into the city of Moscow. In the car, James told me that he had gotten stuck in a large traffic jam leading up to the arrivals section of the airport. He finally abandoned his car, as several others had already done, and ran into the airport to rescue me! He had obviously experienced the Moscow airport himself many times before and knew exactly what I had been subjected to. We both had a good laugh about it after James' profound apologies.

We arrived at James' house, adjacent to the construction of the new church he was assisting with. The house had only three rooms: a bedroom and a toilet upstairs, and a downstairs kitchen with a bed against the front wall. It did have a nice little porch in front with landscaping of six-foot-tall weeds surrounding it. The kitchen was my quarters for the next few days.

After dinner that evening at Red Square, James and I found ourselves pulling a young man off of his grandmother as a crowd of onlookers just stood and watched him beat her in the face with his fists. I suppose he would have continued had James and I not intervened. Moscow, at the time, was a very dark place, full of corruption and teenage alcoholism. Just walking down the tourist area of Red Square that night, almost everyone (mostly young people) had bottles of vodka in their hands, talking in loud boisterous refrains and walking aimlessly with no apparent purpose. I went to bed that night just thinking of the hopelessness of the people of Russia and how much they needed Christ! I was thankful James and Susan were there to minister to the Russian people.

I'll not soon forget the Moscow prison that James and I visited the next day. I have been in many prisons in America, Brazil, and even Mexico, but this one had to be the worst. The men had only lightweight scrubs and flip-flops to wear, with tattered mattresses as bedding. They had one open window, two foot square with bars, which looked out to the prison yard. The concrete room was a small, eighteen-foot-square space with six cement bunk beds surrounding three of the walls. There was an open shower with a single dripping showerhead and a toilet, and one picnic table in the center of the room which was crawling with lice. Each man was allowed one five-minute walk a day, down the dark, narrow two-hundred-foot hallway, while bound hand and foot.

We spent about two hours in the cell with twelve men, talking and trying to give them hope. We shared a hot meal which we had brought with us with them, and then we spent time listening to their gripping stories of despair and hopelessness. The usual one meal a day arrived while we were there in the cell. It consisted of lukewarm broth and a piece of hard, dry bread for each man.

The men seemed very grateful for our message and that we would even take the time to come see them. We shared the gospel and saw all twelve men receive Christ. On our way out, we passed a cell of three Australian tourists who had supposedly broken a traffic law over a year before. They had not been given permission to contact their families or even an attorney, and they handed us a note, requesting that we mail it for them, which we did.

We finally left the prison, and the remainder of my time in Russia was spent laying brick and hauling trash at the construction site of a new church in southern Moscow. After a rough start, but a great and enlightening week of ministry, it was time to return home.

Moscow and the tremendous needs of a former government-controlled nation were overwhelming to me. It was hard to wrap my mind around the need. The building of a church was a good start, but all I could think of was the complacency of the American church and the tendency to become inward and selfish. If this was the future of the church in Moscow, the people as a whole would *never* be reached! I wanted so badly to go back to my church and recruit whoever would volunteer for a team to join James and Susan in their vision to reach Moscow, but I knew it might never happen.

My discouragement and lack of hope dated back to a decision made just a few months' prior. The church in Borger was ending a fund drive to remodel the auditorium. Paint was beginning to peel in places, the carpet was fading, and pews were in need of repair. Plans were made to change the stage and also install soundproofing to lessen the poor acoustics of the large building. These were all legitimate needs, and the church had raised most of the proposed $600,000 needed and was just weeks away from the renovation start.

During the fund-raising period, James and Nikolai, the pastor of the church in Moscow that was being built, made a visit to Borger. Our pastor invited Nikolai to preach on a Sunday morning and share about the work that he was beginning. Nikolai explained that they were nearing the completion of the church but were still trusting God to provide to finish the project. In a question-and-answer period that morning, the question was asked: how much was needed for his church to be fully functional and ready to begin ministry in Moscow? Nikolai answered, "About $600,000 USD."

Immediately following the service, groups of members began forming all over the auditorium discussing the possibility of using our remodel money to finish the Moscow church. It seemed like a perfectly selfless and God-honoring idea. I remember ladies squeaking with excitement as the groups conversed, and discussions centered on how to make it happen. People were coming to me and other staff members asking with excitement, "Can we give the renovation money to Nikolai and help them finish their church? We can delay our needs until later!" This was the heart of many in our congregation, which excited me as well. I encouraged them to approach the proper committee because I didn't want to speak for them.

I don't know what transpired from those group discussions, but I do know that it was announced to the church that evening that the remodel funds could not be used because they were designated funds and the permission of every giver would need to be given. I understood the decision, but I felt like we had missed God by not finding a way to act on the obvious heart of the people.

This was one factor contributing to my overall lack of excitement and the lackluster attitude I had toward God. The resolution was why I ended up in Moscow anyway; I was sent with $10,000, a substantial gift, for Nikolai toward their building fund. It was a generous gift, but I felt it was a compromise from what God really wanted. I don't blame the church—they were following IRS rules—but sometimes it seems we allow technicalities to dictate ministry.

Ironically, I was doing much the same in my relationship with God. I was allowing these circumstances to dictate my relationship to Him. An analogy comes to mind here. Traveling to Moscow, or Hong Kong, is a journey to an exciting and life-changing destination, but the long economy-class flights tend to steal the joy of the trip. Likewise, we travel through the imperfect church on the journey of God's plan for us, and that can sometimes steal our joy on the way to His perfect destination. Nevertheless, the church is the vehicle God chooses to use.

I was not the only one struggling to trust and experience God at that time. My wife, Becky, also wrote about those days.

Becky's Journal (A Different Perspective)

In 1998, the first of our four children, Matthew, was twenty years old and entering his second year of college, his first year at West Texas State A&M in Canyon, Texas. Amy was nineteen years old and entering her first year of college at the same school. She had gone to Budapest with Andy and was a part of the drama team. David was sixteen. These first three kids had all celebrated their birthdays that week—Matt and David with me in Borger and Amy with her dad in Budapest. Our fourth child, Zach, was thirteen years old. I was a stay-at-home mom, and money was very tight. Andy had become the missions pastor at our church after being a youth minister there for ten years. I was asking God to provide for us— for college funds for our first two kids, a car for David, and the list goes on and on. Our needs were great at that point in our lives, and fear was strangling me.

I met with three friends, Jodina, Liz, and Tere, twice a week to pray. We would meet at Travelers Oil (the business belonging to Tere's husband) at 5:30 in the morning so we would have enough time to seriously pray but still be able to get home and get our kids off to school. We were all very needy at the time, and we had a deep longing to hear God and know His direction for our lives. When we started praying together, we all agreed that if anyone couldn't make it for a prayer time, there would be no guilt. But our prayer times were nailed down in stone at 5:30 a.m. on Tuesdays and Thursdays. For the most part, we were all there each time. Occasionally, one of us would have to miss. Our bond had grown through years of praying together and walking with one another through our various crises. We trusted one another.

On this day, I met to pray with Jodina and Tere. I told them I knew something was wrong with my attitude toward our twice-weekly prayer times. I had reread *Fresh Wind, Fresh Fire* by Jim Cymbala, and I saw it! I was no longer desperate. I was no longer desperate for God and had no hope that my circumstances were going to change. We began crying out together, and I confessed to them and God where I was—and where I needed to be. And I began to let go. I let go of my fears, my insecurity, and my hopelessness. As I let go, I felt like I was letting go of a loved one who had already died but one in whom I still found security.

"Forgive me for clinging, God, and not trusting You—trusting that Your plan is good! Unfold Your plan now. I take my fingers out of my ears so I can hear clearly. I let go. Call me out to where You want. Don't let Andy and me miss You. Speak clearly to Andy today. Do a defining work in his life while he's in Russia. I trust you to move in all of our lives—to call all of us (including our kids). Prepare us for Your good plan. I feel loosed from a bondage of desperately clinging to death. Remove fear or dread of the future, God. Bind it from me and my family. Be our hope. Speak clearly to Andy and me—bring us into agreement. Help him to let go too."

This was written just twenty-seven hours before we encountered one of the most incredible experiences of our lives—one where we both became desperate.

The privileges that God had given me at this point in my life were many: traveling the world, being on stage with many famous people, singing to crowds of thirty and forty thousand, and seeing people touched by the gospel. But the experience I was about to have would change my life forever!

Reflecting on my walk at this point in my life, there was no doubt that I knew God, and I had seen Him do many wonderful and amazing things. I knew that He answered prayer and that He was real. I spent time reading His Word and seeking His will in my life, but what was lacking was about to be revealed to me in a profound and unforgettable manner. I was at the place where many Christians and assuredly non-Christians find themselves. The only way I know to say it is similar to the old Wendy's line of the 1980s: "Where's the beef?" My spiritual feelings at the time could be expressed as, "Where's the life?" I certainly knew that, with the exception of the local believers whom I had just met with James and Susan, most of Moscow needed a Savior! And yet, my own faith felt lacking and lifeless. But the truth was, I had the Savior. What I was in search of, I would soon find.

CHAPTER 5

I Never Saw It Coming

On August 7 of 1998, I was to travel from Moscow to New York, but my flight schedule took me back through Budapest for a one-night layover. August 7 was a day to remember for two reasons. One was the terrorist attack on our US embassies in Kenya and Tanzania, in which hundreds of people were killed in simultaneous truck bomb explosions. The other reason, much less earth-shaking but far more personal to me, was my kidnapping. The word of the embassy bombings had not made the news thus far in either the Budapest or Moscow airports in which I was traveling, so I was unaware of the events worldwide.

My main focus when reaching Budapest was to shop for my daughter. Amy had been part of the drama team the week before. She had admired a doll in the window of one of the Váci Utca stores one day as we passed by. Knowing that I would be back in Budapest, I planned to buy the doll for her. We had celebrated her nineteenth birthday in Budapest the week before. Sometimes I'm very unaware of obvious opportunities, but when my daughter had seen the doll, I made a mental note to buy it for her and surprise her when I got home. I was so proud of my thoughtfulness. Note to self: "Pride cometh before a fall!"

I arrived at my hostel from the airport about five o'clock that evening. We had stayed at this same hostel for five summers in a row, so I was very comfortable and familiar with the situation. I took a quick shower and decided to go immediately, before dark, to the Váci Utca area of Budapest to find the doll for Amy.

The Váci Utca area was a short four-block walk and then a ten-minute subway ride from my hostel. One of the assignments each team member had during the weeks of the drama was to take the responsibility to get us from place to place on the subway. This was a great teaching tool for each student, though the consequence was not always arriving at just the right place each time. Now it was my turn to ride alone on the subway and arrive at my proper destination.

Váci Utca is the downtown tourist street, lined with gaslights and shops, which leads to the city square and fountain. The Váci Utca fountain area was one of the favorite places for our team to perform the drama because it drew some of the largest crowds. People of all languages fill the sidewalks of Budapest's Váci Utca (or Váci Street), enjoying the picturesque and ornate architecture and the charming stores. The night I returned from Moscow was no different; as I came up out of the subway, Váci Utca was crowded, alive, and invigorating.

I've never felt comfortable carrying cash when I travel alone, especially on the jam-packed subways, which are always shoulder to shoulder with people. So I only took with me the equivalent of eighty US dollars in forint (Hungarian currency). Being at the end of my three-week trip in Europe, my cash was limited anyway, and I think that was all I had left. The doll was going to be about forty dollars, and I wanted to grab something to eat while I was out as well.

I found the doll at Váci Utca, but as it was in the main tourist section of the city, I thought I might find the same doll cheaper along the Danube River where the outdoor night market was set up. I walked the six or so blocks to the river market and found the same doll at a much lower price.

My next decision set in motion an experience that could have potentially cost my own life.

Instead of carrying the doll around with me, I decided to find a place to eat nearby and purchase the doll on my way back to the hostel. I walked for several blocks before I found a place that I thought was a restaurant. A lady was standing behind a podium wearing a white shirt and black pants, and her daughter was playing on a bench next to her. To me it seemed like a safe place, so I asked, "Resturante?" and she replied, "Igan" (yes).

I followed her into the building. All I could see was her white shirt as I walked behind her through the pitch-black room. Even after several minutes, when my eyes finally adjusted, the room was still very dark, and as far as I could determine, I was the only person in the entire place. I was used to restaurants in Budapest having a bar as you first entered, and being escorted past the bar to the rear of the building where most of the eating patrons would be seated. The restaurants were usually smoke-filled and dimly lit, but not nearly to the extent of this establishment.

Restaurants in Budapest were normally very loud and crowded, so my first thought was that this might not be one of the better places. Then I thought it might be so quiet because it was not near the touristy Váci Utca district; rather, it was nearer the quiet river walk. It took a minute or so before I saw anyone else once I was ushered to my table.

I was seated at the back of the room, against the wall, on a bench seat. The only light came from what looked like the kitchen area about twenty feet from my table. I remember the room being very cold compared to the warm, humid evening of Budapest.

Shortly, the lady returned to take my drink order, but by that time I was beginning to feel very uncomfortable about the situation. I thought about just walking out after my eyes had adjusted, but I wasn't sure where the entrance was. I reluctantly ordered a Coke, but I had already decided to leave as soon as I drank it. Being alone in a cold dark building which I knew nothing about made me question my decision to even enter the restaurant. Over the five years of traveling to Budapest, I had let my guard down and become comfortable. But now I was beginning to recall the warning from the first year to be careful of unfamiliar places. I was hoping this was not one of those places!

The lady returned with a can and a glass of ice which I had requested (two cubes in Europe, if you're lucky), and she began to pour the drink into the glass. I took a sip and immediately knew that she had brought me a beer and not a Coke. I began explaining to her that I had ordered a Coke, not a beer.

At that point, people began coming out of the woodwork. Another girl with a cocktail-looking drink in her hand slid in next to me on the bench and asked if I needed interpretation. I was relieved that someone spoke English and that I could get the problem resolved. I turned to explain to her about the mix-up, and another girl, also with a drink in hand, slid in on the right side of me. It was then that I really knew something was wrong! I told the "interpreter," on my left, that I wanted the waitress to just bring me the check and I would leave.

As I waited for the check, the girls asked me questions. Where was I from? How long had I been in Budapest? What was my job? At this point, I was becoming very leery of telling them anything about myself. The waitress finally brought the check, and at first, I thought I was seeing it incorrectly. The bill read 92,480 forint. That was the equivalent of five hundred US dollars! I knew something was wrong, but all I could do was go into defense mode. I didn't have the $500, and I knew I didn't owe it. I also knew that I was now being set up in some way.

As I began showing my disagreement, out came a stocky, well-dressed man wearing a suit and a newsboy cap. His wide nose took a couple turns and filled his hard face as he looked at me with his dark, recessed eyes. Leaning down against my table he said in a deep voice, "Problem?"

Hoping he didn't have a gun under his coat, I explained the problem once again, but he insisted that I must pay the bill. We argued back and forth for several seconds through the interpreter, and I finally asked him how a Coke, or in this case a beer, could even cost that much? Then he explained to me that I was buying the two girls' drinks as well. I told him that I never asked the girls to sit with me, and for that matter never offered to buy their drinks. I never even knew anyone else was in the building besides me and the waitress!

"I am *not* paying for their drinks," I shouted.

At that time, as if on cue, out came another man from the darkness. As I began to scoot the girl on my right over so I could stand, I told them they could have forty forint and I was leaving.

The two men shoved me back down and demanded again that I pay the amount of the check. My heart sank, and a feeling of fear and helplessness set in. I gave them what I had and said, "That's it, and I have no more!" They insisted that I use my credit card, but I told them I didn't have one with me. The interpreter exclaimed, "All travelers have credit cards!", and then she declared that we would go to my hotel to get them.

I listened in disbelief. I had little hope that they were going to change their minds, and I had no answers of how to solve the dilemma. My only plan was escape, but then I thought, *If I go to the police, I will be accused of nonpayment and walking the ticket. It will be my word against theirs.* There was continued conversation, disagreement, argument, and reasoning. The moment was too intense to pray or even really think.

Little did I know that it was about to get worse.

CHAPTER 6
EVERYTHING CHANGES

The man in the suit called someone on his radio and informed me that we would be going to my hotel to get my credit card. I thought, *I can lose them on the subway, and at least I will be out in public where I might find some help.* I began planning to go down into the subway and jump on the first train with an open door. It was always very crowded as people entered and left each car. Like most subways, there were always trains traveling in two directions, so I would take the first open train and figure out where I was later. I knew the subway system fairly well. Even if any of my captors made the train with me, I could push my way through all of the passengers back to another car and maybe lose them by the next stop. I thought it was my best chance.

I didn't know what these people were capable of at this point, but I knew the suit guy was serious. He didn't smile, flinch, or give any indication of compromise. I also assumed that he might have a gun under his suit coat. Because they didn't call the police about my "unpaid bill," I determined that they knew they were wrong and didn't care.

My first plan was to make a break for it as we left the restaurant, but within seconds, another man walked in the building and helped everyone escort me to a very small taxi, sitting on the curb just inches from the front door of the building. They stuffed me in the backseat with the two girls and the other man while the driver and the suit guy rode in front, and off we went speeding to the hostel. My best chance of escape was lost, and the possibilities were suddenly more limited. My thoughts now turned to keeping them away from my hostel. If they discovered where I was staying, what would I do then?

Being in a car dashed my initial plans, so my hope turned to escaping from the taxi at the first opportunity. I really thought there would be a chance to jump out over the interpreter if we slowed down or came to a stop. She was a very small, petite girl, and she was wearing a dress and heels, so I thought it should be fairly easy to get past her. I didn't give them the address of my hostel, only the sector that it was in, hoping to escape before we arrived there.

Since I didn't know how to get to my hostel by car, I gave them the nearest subway exit name. My brain was racing…I had to get out of the taxi! The driver sped through the narrow and busy streets of Budapest, running red lights, honking his horn, and never giving me a chance to jump out. I continued to hope for a chance to escape, but the opportunity never came.

Since they had gone to the trouble of renting a taxi, I knew they must be serious about getting the money. I began to wonder *how* serious. Would they hurt me or even kill me? I didn't know, but both possibilities were running through my mind. Soon we arrived at the subway exit, and they demanded that I show them where I was staying. I knew they all had radios because they had used them at the restaurant earlier, and I assumed they might have guns as well. I didn't know, and I didn't want to find out!

When we got to the hostel, the driver drove within inches of the chain-link gate surrounding the front of the building. Standing there was the seventy-two-year-old night watchman with eyes wide open.

With fear in his voice, he asked me, "Andy, what is wrong?"

I told him, "Nothing, it's okay."

Everything within me wanted to tell him that I was in trouble, but I didn't know how, and I just felt it wasn't the right time. The thoughts continued to run through my mind whether this or that would get me killed, or would now or later be the best time to try to make an escape. I wanted to stay alive, and whatever accomplished that was what I would do. I didn't want the old man to be harmed, and besides, he didn't speak enough English to understand me. He had been at this hostel for the past five summers working as a night clerk and watchman, and despite his lack of English had become a friend. His small frame and distinguished white hair even reminded me a little of my Grandpa Byrns.

Many well-meaning people have told me what they would have done in my situation. Several people have said, "I wouldn't have gone in a restaurant I knew nothing about." Others, mainly men, have said, "I would have gotten up and left…just let them try to stop me!" Another comment has been, "Seems like it would have been pretty easy to run once you were outside." Believe me, all those thoughts crossed my mind many times, but when my life became the ransom, it wasn't a bet I was willing to make. "Had that been me, this is what I would have done!" I've said that so many times when judging others and the decisions they make. It is easy to give advice, or to say how one would handle certain situations, but until you have *been there*, you really *don't* know how you would handle it! Needless to say, my perspective has changed much since being kidnapped in Budapest. Another lesson learned: don't judge someone in whose shoes you've not walked.

The hostel was actually a three-story college dorm that was used to house tourists during the summer. I was the only resident there that night because the dorm was going to close for the season, but they had kept it open one extra night just for me. Right inside the front door, looking through a window, was the watchman's room with a bed and TV, and on his wall were all the room keys. I asked him for my key, and then all six of us headed through the lobby and down the long hall to my room.

I knew as we took those steps that my situation had grown more dangerous again. *Now they know where I'm staying. Even if I get away, they could find me again.* My hope at that point was that the old man would call the police, and they would be waiting at the front of the hostel when we came back out. Yet, even that scenario scared me, because these people had radios and could easily let their friends know what was happening. Was I afraid to die? No. Was I afraid to be killed? *Yes!* Most of us think about dying, but from old age or a disease, and with our loved ones around us. Being killed is somewhat more unnerving. In the movies it's never a pleasant thing; plus, it normally happens alone and is sometimes cruel. I tried not to let my mind go there, but I couldn't slow the thoughts of this possibly happening.

When we arrived at my room, I opened my locker just inside the door and retrieved my credit cards. As we headed down the hall and back to the lobby, I was praying that the police would be there waiting. No such luck. The old man was cowering in his quarters, with his trembling hand reaching out through the sliding window for my key. I will never forget the look of concern and fear in his eyes when he looked back at me as we hurried out to the waiting taxi. Another missed chance to be rescued!

After being stuffed back into the taxi, a new fear suddenly hit me…how were the credit cards going to help me? The sun was beginning to set behind the skyline of Budapest, and darkness was my opponent and their ally. At sunset, I doubted that any banks would still be open. I think this was my greatest point of fear in the whole ordeal so far. Were they taking me to an

ATM machine? If so, I didn't know my PIN number! In 1998, few people in the United States used a PIN (especially for credit cards), and I certainly didn't know mine. Again, my mind started racing: Was it my birth date? Was it my anniversary? Was it something simple that I should remember? My only hope was that they were headed to an open bank. What would be their response to me if I couldn't use an ATM? Would that be the final thing to push them to harm me? We were now in a less traveled area of the city, and the potential for the group to harm me was greater and much less open to the public eye.

After a mile or so, we turned the corner, and my fears came true: they pulled up to an ATM machine. At this point, I didn't know for sure where I was, and it was just beginning to get dark. I told the kidnappers that I didn't know my PIN number but that I would give it a try. The interpreter shouted, "Everyone knows their PIN number!" That was true; everyone in Hungary knew their PIN number because, at that time, Hungary had already gone to the debit card system. The United States, however, was just beginning to launch that format.

They pushed me up to the machine, and it was very hard to see the dark screen from the glare of the setting sun behind me. This area of the city had no other people around except for passing cars and taxis. I began to enter numbers...nothing worked. I must have tried six or seven times, and still nothing. I knew this was futile. I couldn't even remember giving the bank a PIN when we first opened our account. I didn't think we actually had one.

Then the man in the suit began screaming at me. I turned to the interpreter to ask what he was saying, and she explained that he was very angry. That I could see—she didn't need to tell me! Occasionally the man would blurt out an English word or two, but mostly it would be interpreted. After several failed tries,

I told her that this was not going to work, but if we could find an open bank, I could get the money.

She turned to the suit guy and began explaining the problem. He screamed out, "There are no banks open now!" But the interpreter said, "I know of one!" So they threw me back in the taxi and we headed down the busy streets again, speeding, honking, and dodging oncoming cars. I was hoping to find a way to escape, but knowing they had radios, and not knowing for sure where I was, I decided it was best to wait.

Again, at this point I was hoping for a way of escape, looking for an open door or even a giving up on the part of the captors. My thoughts were on escape as the interpreter occasionally injected comments or questions. I suppose I was unconsciously praying, but I don't remember a literal prayer—the situation was simply too intense. God, however, would soon find a way to bring prayer into the story—and to show me that He was still in control.

CHAPTER 7

THE GROUP GETS BIGGER

Within fifteen minutes or so, we were back near Váci Utca, the area I knew best in Budapest. As we drove up and exited the car, I noticed that several more people had joined their group, which increased the number to six or seven men and three girls. This was going to make it even harder to get away, not to mention that they seemed to know almost everyone we saw. They would speak to, and many times shake the hands of, those they passed. Many of the acquaintances would turn and walk with us, especially as we walked down busy Váci Utca.

We walked in a tight group about two blocks from the street to the bank. They shuffled me up to the window, surrounding me on each side, and pushed my head down toward the opening of the teller's booth. I gave him my personal American Express card and asked for $100.

The teller, who spoke English, explained that they didn't take American Express, only Visa and MasterCard. ("American Express, don't leave home without it"?) Thankfully, the other card I had with me was a MasterCard—the only problem being that it was not my card; it belonged to the church.

I slid the card to the teller, only to find out a few seconds later that the card was denied. It was over the limit! At the time, the church had only one card for all six staff members to use, and it had a monthly limit of one thousand dollars. I learned later that the card had been used for large Vacation Bible School purchases prior to my leaving for Europe. This angered the suit guy once again. It angered me too! Still, I felt a glimmer of hope. *Okay, since my cards don't work, maybe they will forget the whole thing and leave me alone.* At the same time, I feared it could also accelerate my demise.

Their actions quickly dashed any hopes. They wanted the money, and it seemed they were willing to do anything to get it. The only thing I could think of was to ask if they would let me make a phone call to get my PIN number. The interpreter turned to the suit guy and repeated my offer. He nodded his head yes and pointed back down Váci Utca.

I had used the PIN number only as a stall tactic, hoping they would finally give up. I doubted any person back home would know the PIN anyway. If anyone would know the number, it would be our administrator, Dixie. She was a very organized and efficient person, but unfortunately didn't have authority over the card limit. I began to wonder how I was going to make the call—I didn't have an international calling card, and I didn't see a phone around anywhere.

This is when everything began to change. My captors walked me about three blocks down busy Váci Utca to an outdoor pay phone on the wall. A man was leaning against the wall, in conversation on the phone, when the suit guy just grabbed the phone from him, shoved him aside, and handed the phone to me. Wow, that took both me and the man by surprise!

Now, *everyone* on the street was watching the whole thing, and people gathered around to observe. The locals seemed to know what was happening and who my captors were. This made me think that these people were not to be messed with. Everyone acted as though they didn't want to get involved; even the guy using the phone just put his hands in the air and stepped back. Had someone jerked the phone out of my hands and shoved me aside, it would have been hard for me to just step back and surrender unless I already knew of their reputation. I felt some empathy from the bystanders, but I also saw the fear on their faces and their reluctance to intervene.

I knew the call was going to surprise my wife, because we seldom called one another when traveling out of the country. I attempted to make the call, but the interpreter told me that I must have a calling card. I responded, "I don't have one with me."

The suit guy handed me his calling card, so I put it in the phone. The recorded message said, "Please enter your country calling code." Then it dawned on me that I didn't know my country calling code. I remembered seeing 011 somewhere, so I tried it, plus my home number. Surprisingly, it worked! Now... what was I going to tell my wife?

After several rings, I waited nervously, hoping she would answer. Connecting with Becky might be my only hope of a solution. To my great relief, she finally answered. Her tone was happy and surprised to hear from me. I didn't want to scare her or cause any more fear than necessary, so I tried to sound calm and confident. I wanted to convey urgency, but not to the point that she would panic and not be able to function. Becky is generally a very rational person, but if panicked, her ability to make wise decisions can sometimes be drastically impaired.

"How are you?' she asked warmly.

I replied, "I'm good. Listen to me, I have a little problem, but I think I'll be okay. I've been taken by a group, and they want money from me. I think they will let me go if I can give them what they want, but I need our PIN number. I also need you to call and see why I can't withdraw money from the church credit card."

She understandably began asking questions, so I told her the people were surrounding me and I would try to call her back soon. I could hear her digging in a panic, searching through papers and opening drawers, looking for our PIN. She could not locate it anywhere. The problem now would be difficulty in reaching her if I tried to call back—would the line be busy, would I miss her, and would I even get another chance to make a call? So I told her to put the phone down and run next door to call the church. I whispered, "You need to hurry!"

She came back in about two minutes and told me that our church business secretary would have to call the bank to get the number. I also asked her to search for a local Western Union in Budapest, and told her that she could give me that information when I called back.

"I love you, and I will call you back as soon as I can. Don't worry, I will be okay!"

Becky's Journal (A Different Perspective)

On Friday morning, August 7, Amy, David, and Zach decided to go to Canyon to spend the night. Matt was already living there, and the boys wanted to go hang out with him. Amy was meeting her roommate at the dorm, and they were going to move some of their things in. I'd really wanted to go along, but I knew that I'd be able to get the house clean before Andy got home if I stayed. I also relished having a little "alone time," which was very unusual with four kids. So after the kids left, I began cleaning house. My goal was to get as much done as possible before lunch and then treat myself with takeout from The Plaza, our favorite local restaurant. Amy had already been home from Budapest about a week, and Andy was on the last leg of his trip home from Russia—where he'd gone after Budapest.

I'd already ordered my lunch when I got a phone

call from Andy. It was very unusual for Andy to call me when he was out of the country…it was just too expensive. So I was excited to hear from him. He told me he'd gone to a restaurant to eat dinner and he really couldn't understand the people, but they were demanding $500 and it was serious. He needed the PIN number for our credit card. I had a million questions, but Andy told me to hurry—so I began digging through our rolltop desk where I kept our important papers. I found all the papers from our credit card company, but there was no PIN number. I ran back to the kitchen phone to tell him I couldn't find one. He couldn't hang up, so he told me to run next door to our neighbor's house and use their phone to call Dixie, our church's financial secretary, and see if she knew the PIN number to the church's credit card. I ran! I didn't even know these new neighbors, but I banged on the door and hurriedly explained that I needed to use their phone.

I called Dixie and told her that Andy was in trouble and needed the PIN number to the church's credit card. She quickly looked for it and came back on the line to tell me she didn't have it and would have to call the bank to get it. I ran back to our house and told Andy what Dixie was doing and that I hadn't thought of calling our bank, so I was going to take our credit card information back to the neighbor's house and do the same thing. So I did. I ran back to the neighbor's house and called the company to see if they would give me our PIN number. They wouldn't. Because the card was under Andy's name, I couldn't get the information.

As I was leaving the neighbors' house, they told me that I could come back and use their phone if I needed to. They knew from hearing my conversations what was going on. I was afraid Andy wouldn't be on the line when I got back to our phone, but he was. I explained what was going on, and he was very frustrated—and I began to hear real fear in his voice. Then he asked me to find out if there was a Western Union in Budapest, and I told him I would—but to give me some time. He told me he loved me and we hung up.

I immediately called Western Union and found out there was only one Western Union in all of Budapest, Hungary…and that it probably closed at 6:00 p.m. It was already later than that in Budapest. I was shaken but realized I still had food waiting at The Plaza. I wasn't thinking rationally, but being the responsible person I am, I jumped in my car and took off for the restaurant to get the food I'd ordered! As I drove like a madwoman, I was trying to figure out what was going on. All I really knew at that point was that we were going to have to pay $500 that we didn't have. It made me sick to my stomach. We desperately needed that money for tuition—not to pay for a mistake! I hurried home and opened my food and found that I couldn't even eat, so I took the food to my kitchen counter and left it untouched. And I began to panic. I fell on my knees in front of my couch, crying out to God and asking Him to spare Andy's life. I opened my Bible to Psalm 91 and prayed it as a prayer over Andy.

I called Jodina and Kaye, another genuine friend. I told them that Andy was in serious trouble and I just needed someone to be with me. I knew they could drive across our small town and be there in five minutes. But the first person to show up at my door that day was Les, our youth minister. Dixie had advised the entire church staff about what was going on after she'd gotten my phone call. So Les came. Jodina and Kaye were close behind him. I told them all what I knew, and Jodina went outside to call our prayer partners so they could come.

Les prayed with Kaye and me. The first thing he prayed was, "God, bring in Your order." I prayed in agreement. And at that moment, my heart was filled with an unnatural peace. It was almost a surreal experience, with strangely calm thoughts going on in my mind as the next events took place.

After I hung up the phone, I told the interpreter that we needed to go back to the bank. She didn't understand that I had *not* gotten a PIN number. I was hoping going back there would buy me some time, and I could escape before we got back to the bank. It was still daylight in Texas, but it was now dark in Budapest.

By this time, the group had grown by three or four more men and one couple. As we walked, the new girl slid her arm inside mine and laughingly asked me if I wanted to "party" with her. The boyfriend, screaming, grabbed her by the hair and threw her to the ground. I certainly didn't desire to make someone else mad at me! I thought, *If he would do that to his girlfriend, what will he do to me?* For a moment the couple left the group, yelling at one another and obviously angry with me.

As I remember all the variables in that situation, the angry people, the difficulty getting the money they wanted, and the obvious frustrations, I can see now how God was taking care of me. They could have decided far sooner to end this ordeal, yet God protected me, even with the *surprise* that was about to come.

CHAPTER 8

"Now You Die!"

After struggling through the growing night crowd, we finally made our way near the sidewalk bank. *What will they do when they discover that I don't have a number?* I wondered. *I need to get away if possible, but they have me surrounded.*

Just that quickly, we were back at the bank. I didn't have a PIN number, and I didn't have a different card, so all I could do was ask the teller to run the declined card one more time. I knew my chances of it being approved were zero, but it was all I had. As I handed the card back to the teller, I could see the disgust on his face as he refused to run it again.

When the suit guy saw this, he slammed his fist on the counter and screamed out an angry sentence. I asked the interpreter what he said, and she told me, "Now the bad!"

I said, "Now the bad; what is that?"

She whispered, "Now you die!"

All along, this thought had been in my mind. I'd felt that it could happen; that at any moment, things might go that badly. But to hear it verbalized sent chills up my spine. I immediately began explaining, "My wife is in the process of getting the PIN number, and if I can make *one more* phone call, I can give you the money that you want!"

The interpreter turned to explain this to the suit guy. Still angry, the man shouted, "One more, that is it!"

Then we turned and walked, in a tight group, several blocks away…this time through the square and past the fountain to a lone phone booth away from busy Váci Utca. Each time we walked and moved away from the crowd of tourists, I would begin to feel a loss of security. I felt that I was safer as long as we were in a crowd. This area was a busy place during the day but was empty and poorly lit at night, and my fears grew stronger.

They put me in the phone booth, and I began making my second phone call home. This time when I called, about forty-five minutes after the first call, I heard a room full of voices in the background. My wife told me that many people were making phone calls, praying, and helping in any way they could. We were blessed with loving and close friends in Borger, and my heart was touched as I heard their heartfelt efforts to help.

Then she asked how I was doing, and I told her I thought I could get away, but it was a matter of time. I asked her if she had found out about the church card, and she told me that she had talked to the bank president and that he had approved whatever I needed, so I should run the card again. My thought was, *I would rather have a PIN number than just the word of a bank president before I use the same card again!*

She also told me there was only one Western Union in Budapest, but it closed at 6 p.m., and she wasn't sure where it was located. Then she told me that the Budapest police had been contacted and were looking for me.

"The local US ambassador has also been informed, but the embassy isn't going to be able to help you because two embassies in Africa have been attacked today, and *all* US embassies are now on alert."

She also told me that a US congressman and a US congress-woman from Texas were aware of my dilemma and were doing what they could to help.

Becky's Journal [A Different Perspective]

Tere and Liz got to my house, and they immediately

went to my bedroom with Kaye and began to pray. Now, my friends and I were used to doing battle in prayer at Travelers Oil, and we didn't usually do it quietly. So they were crying before the throne of grace on Andy's behalf when our pastor arrived. And our pastor wasn't used to loud praying. It was one of those moments when I was chuckling on the inside, knowing my friends would be mortified if they knew our pastor could hear their loud petitioning. I don't know if they heard him or someone clued them in, but they came through the living room telling me they were going to move the prayer meeting to the church and call others to come pray with them. I didn't know until the next day that dozens of people were at the church praying together…and some even came without knowing a prayer meeting was going on. They just wanted to get to the church to pray for Andy.

Things were happening quickly. I knew I needed to call Andy's parents so they would know what was going on and then let my own parents know about the situation. Those were the only two phone calls I made. I was afraid to use my phone for fear I'd miss Andy's next call. Jodina stepped outside again and called AT&T and had emergency call-waiting set up on my phone just so I wouldn't miss his calls.

I had no idea how quickly word had already spread. Friends, church secretaries, church members, and family were calling senators, the State Department, local officials, and the Baptist Foreign Mission Board. Little by little, people were showing up at my small (but clean!) three-bedroom house to see what was going on. A friend in our church was sister to Congressman Larry

Combest, and she called him for his help. Leon, a lawyer and church friend, e-mailed Congressmen Mac Thornberry and Phil Gramm, while another contacted the FBI about Andy's situation. Some of these people had cell phones and were sitting in my living room doing their calling, although cell phones were not in wide circulation at that time. The police came to my house, and I signed to have a trace put on my phone. I wasn't sure what they could do from so far away, but I wanted to do whatever I could from my end.

And then my phone rang.

It was Andy, for the second time. I quickly told him what was going on and that there was a Western Union in Budapest, but the operator I'd talked to thought it closed at 6 p.m. I also told him that the bank president (who also went to our church) had told Dixie he would open a line of unlimited credit on the church credit card, and if Andy ran it again, there would be money available to him. He knew it was an emergency and promised money would be there.

I told Andy everyone was praying and urged him to remember Psalm 91. He told me, "Becky, I can't even think right now! I'm just trying to survive here." I assured him that we were praying and claiming that Scripture for him. And at this point, we never hung up again without saying, "I love you!"

Becky's words were encouraging, yet they gave me little hope. It was good to know that people were trying to help me, but I honestly couldn't see how someone all the way in Texas would be helpful in Budapest, especially in light of the embassy being shut down. I assumed that, if I was going to be free, no one else could do it for me. I knew God would have to open a door, and I would have to *run* through it. It wouldn't be the first time God had made a way of escape in my life.

After I hung up, I asked the interpreter if she knew where the Western Union was. She replied, "Western Union; what's Western Union?"

I tried to explain to her without any response. She kept saying, "I don't know Western Union."

I explained to her that a Western Union could wire me money if we could find one. I said, "Western Unions are worldwide, and my wife said there *is* one in Budapest!" I turned and looked through the yellow pages in the phone booth with no result. Finding the *one* Western Union in a city of over two million people would be a miracle, and I really needed a miracle!

Finally, I gave up on the idea. With some trepidation, I informed the interpreter that my bank president would make the card good and that we needed to go back to the bank. So we walked the four or five blocks back to the sidewalk bank. I was dreading the response of the teller, and I knew it might mean the end.

As we approached the bank, I saw right above the teller's head a yellow-and-black banner that read, "Western Union, the fastest way to send money!" I couldn't believe I hadn't seen it earlier. I thought, *Okay, God, you are still taking care of me!*

To be honest, things were moving so fast, and the captors were asking so many questions, I didn't have time to really pray. Every thought I had of escape was directed to God, hoping that He would open a door. But I can't say that I really prayed. My thoughts were consumed with finding a way of escape...and living! Now I had proof that He was watching: one Western

Union in all of Budapest, Hungary, and I had already been there two times. *That was God!*

I pointed out the sign to the interpreter, hoping she sensed my genuine attempt to get her the money. Now the thought crossed my mind—was it open? Becky had told me it was already closed, but I had to try.

As I stepped up to the window for the third time, the look on the teller's face said, "Not again?" He was surprised when I asked him if the Western Union was open, but his answer surprised me even more when he said, "Yes."

Thank you, Lord! I thought. *Finally some hope!*

This was the first time I had ever used a Western Union, so I wasn't familiar with the process. The teller handed me a form, so I filled out the information. All seemed well until I reached the bottom of the page. At the bottom was the question, "MTCN control number?" I didn't know what the MTCN control number was, so I left it blank. I just assumed that it was for the bank to fill in.

The bank teller looked at the form and frowned. He told me I had to have a number from the sending party which, of course, would be my wife. Since I didn't have that number, I made one up and told the teller to send it. I then began to doubt that the Western Union thing would work, so I considered what to do in the event it came back declined.

As we waited for the approval from home, I heard a British accent from the window to my right. The interpreter was on my left, so I quietly got the man's attention and whispered that I was an American and had been kidnapped, could he help me? He didn't understand me at first, so I repeated the question. The man looked cautiously back over his left shoulder, eyed the people surrounding me, and said, "Sorry." Then he finished his transaction, said "Good luck," and left. I'm not sure, had the

tables been turned, that I would have known how to help someone in my situation either, especially in a foreign country. I think
I would have at least tried, but it was not to be. There I go saying
what I would have done "had it been me."

About that time, I could see the Western Union response
coming back from the fax machine. The teller walked over to
the machine to retrieve the paper and slid it under the window
to me. It read "Declined." With that, the suit guy became very
angry, as did the interpreter.

I asked the teller what I needed to do to get the proper
MTCN number, and he told me that it had to come from the
person from whom I was requesting the money. I replied, "So if
I have the proper number, you will give me the money?"

"Yes!" he said.

Then I pulled the interpreter's head down to the window
opening and said to the banker, "Tell her!"

At the banker's answer, the interpreter screamed, "One last
call!"

Up until this point, I felt that the interpreter and I had built
a good rapport, and if anything, she was trying to help me. We
had even laughed about something a couple times, but now that
friendly demeanor quickly disappeared. I probably shouldn't
have shoved her head to the window, but I was getting frustrated
as well. Now I felt like my one safety net had deteriorated.

The interpreter and the suit guy began a rather intense dis-
cussion, and then they turned me around and said, "Let's go!"
They didn't tell me where we were going; they just grabbed me,
and off we went into the darkness—and the most frightening
moment yet.

CHAPTER 9

This Is It!

Becky's Journal (A Different Perspective)

Pastor Gregg and Leon were sitting with me during the next interim. Other people were in and out. Because I'd been to Budapest with Andy previously, I could imagine him in my mind walking the streets of Váci Utca, going to the bank and getting the money. Prayers were constantly going through my mind, and it was hard to follow conversations. In hindsight, it was at this point that Satan made a frontal attack on my mind with all kinds of imaginations to draw me into complete and absolute fear. The peace I'd experienced when Les prayed earlier slowly began to dissipate. People I knew and loved were showing up at my house, and it was such a comfort. One of those people was Michael—Jodina's husband. He was there the next time Andy called.

It was the first time Andy or I had ever used Western Union. He told me he'd wired me for money, but it didn't come. He needed a control number. I had no idea what that was or how to get it. I called Western Union in Borger and told the woman there that I needed a control number. She told me I'd have to bring the money to her and get one. I told her it was an emergency—that my husband was being held hostage in Budapest, Hungary, and we needed the control number immediately. She told me to just bring her the money.

Michael knew what was happening and said, "Hand me that phone!" Because Borger is a small town, our Western Union was run by a lady who also had an answering service—which Michael used for his business. He got on the phone and demanded, "Judith! Give the man the money!"

I guess she was convinced, because Michael began giving me a control number. And his voice was loud enough that Andy heard the number before I gave it to him. I could tell Andy was getting fatigued from all of the fear and running from bank to phone booth. I tried to reassure him that the embassy knew what was going on and that they were sending police out to look for him. Again, we ended our conversation with, "I love you."

I'm a pretty confident person, but my confidence was slowly slipping away. How much could the embassy do? I knew there was nothing I could do from across the ocean. It was a very helpless feeling knowing my husband was being held captive in a foreign country. I was totally out of control. And even in the midst of a very crowded house, I felt completely alone. Even though these people loved us, there was nothing they could do to prevent a tragedy from happening. I may have looked pretty calm on the outside, but I was falling apart on the inside as Satan offered me every possible scenario for a bad ending to this story. I never moved from the couch. I could hardly carry on a conversation for my fear. People would walk in and tell me what was going on with the phone calls being made to officials. I knew the embassy was well aware of Andy Dietz in Budapest, Hungary. In fact, we later found out that the ambassador had been called by several officials asking for his help. I knew that he had called the local Hungarian police asking them to be on the lookout for this American.

Again, we started walking down Váci Utca toward the first sidewalk phone, but this time we walked past that phone three or four blocks and turned right toward the river. The further we walked from the gaslights of Váci Utca, the darker it became. The time was somewhere around ten o'clock at night, and I knew the kidnappers had lost patience. I began to wonder how late the bank would stay open, and the words "Now you die!" kept haunting me.

We must have walked five or six blocks and were nearing the river; we had not passed a single person. It seemed that most of the tourists and nightlife were far from where we were. My mind started racing with panic. *I've waited too late, and now they're going to either beat me up or dump me in the Danube. I have to do something; there is no choice.* I felt backed into a corner with no other options. The entire group was walking behind me, so my only option was to run straight ahead into the darkness and hopefully find the night market still busy with tourists.

Just as I was about to make a break for it, the suit guy began shouting at a man approaching us from the dark. As he got closer, I could see muscles bulging out from his skin-tight white T-shirt. He had a long black ponytail and stood about six-three. I thought, *This is the guy who's going to tie me up and dump me in the dirty, cold Danube River.* I had thoughts of the old mob movies where victims were tied with hands behind their backs and cement blocks tied to their feet and dumped alive into the bottom of the Hudson River. *I'm going to die!* I thought. *This is it.*

It was a warm, humid night…but suddenly I was cold. I remember my body beginning to shake and my jaw quivering. I wanted to scream like a girl, but I didn't. As he walked toward us, the suit guy and the muscle guy continued talking and pointing at me. Then the muscle guy pointed to his right at a British-style red-trimmed glass telephone booth under a lone streetlight. They all walked me to the phone booth, shoved me in, handed me the phone card, and shut the squeaking door behind me.

Okay, I have one more chance. I'm so glad I didn't scream! The phone booth became a refuge that I didn't want to leave.

With this call, I felt that we needed to make some significant progress, or my time might run out. No matter the outcome, I had to sell it to the kidnappers just so I could get back to the busy area of Váci Utca where I felt my chances were better. I was glad I was in a phone booth, because the kidnappers couldn't hear my conversation and I would be able to speak freely.

Once again, I slid the phone card in and began dialing my wife's number. I remember the warm phone booth beginning to slow the chill of my body. I didn't know what I was hoping for… just any kind of good news on the other end of the phone. Maybe when I got back to the bank, the police would be there to rescue me…I didn't know.

This was my longest conversation with my wife. It was good to hear her voice again. I knew she was very concerned, but her composure really impressed me under the circumstances. I really needed to sense this following my most intimidating encounter of the night. I knew it had to be God!

She told me to keep watching for the police because they were looking for me and to keep trying the card. I told her that I had found the Western Union at the bank we were using, and she was excited.

"It's open," I said, "but I need a MTCN control number from the sender." I explained that the MTCN number was the number at the bottom of the form and that it had to come from her. "The kidnappers told me that they want $500," I said.

While I waited, Becky got on another phone to call the Borger Western Union, but they wouldn't give her the money unless she went down to the local office. I was overhearing this entire conversation amidst the fifty or so other voices that had gathered in my house, and I heard Becky explain, "This is an emergency; he has been kidnapped!"

Then, with a deep Texas drawl, I heard a voice I would recognize anywhere. "Give me that phone!" It was Michael, a rough oil field worker with a heart of gold. Michael and his wife had become like family to Becky and me, and they would do anything for us. A family crisis had drawn us together, and it was through the crisis that Becky and Jodina had become prayer warriors and as close as sisters. Michael had become a very special friend to me as well, one of those "two o'clock in the morning friends"; a friend I could call at any time if I needed him, and he would be there.

"Judith, give the man the money!" Michael shouted. "Yes, I'll be good for it, just give the man the money!"

It made me chuckle, even under the circumstances. I needed that comic relief, but what I really needed was Michael there with me!

Then I heard Michael repeat a number with his slow Texas drawl, "Niiiine, fooo-ur, thr-eee…"

With the phone pressed between my ear and shoulder, I motioned to the interpreter for a pen and began writing the number on my hand. It was a hot, humid night, so I was hoping the number wouldn't rub off. Then Becky came back on the phone.

"I heard the number!" I said, and I began repeating it back to her just to be sure. I whispered to her that I was going to try to escape, "Just keep praying." It gave me a little hope each time I called home and knew my friends were there trying to support me in any way they could. I knew that I had to give Becky hope too, even though my options were growing slim. I was amazed at how cool and calm she seemed each time I talked to her.

We both told each other "I love you!", and I hung up. I told the kidnappers that I had the number that I needed and that we should be able to get the money now.

CHAPTER 10

THE POLICE TOO?

This time, we made our way back up the five or six blocks away from the river to Váci Utca. I was glad to be walking away from that river! When we got back to the lighted Váci Utca district and were walking toward the bank, I noticed a policeman about thirty feet away, walking toward us through the crowd. I remembered Becky saying that the police were looking for me, so, without being obvious, I began trying to make eye contact with him. I was taller than anyone in the group except for the muscle guy, and he was walking right behind me.

About ten feet from the policeman, I finally caught his eye. There was no doubt that he saw me as I looked at him with my eyes wide open and mouthed, "Help me!" I could see a look of inquiry from the people behind him; my hope was the kidnappers wouldn't notice. I began to feel a sense of real hope for the first time.

The policeman surveyed the people surrounding me, looking to the left and right with fear; then he looked me in the eyes and shook his head "NO." Then he turned and walked away. I couldn't believe it! If the police wouldn't help, what was I going to do? Again, I felt a sense of urgency. My thought was that the policeman was scared or maybe even corrupt, which concerned me. Would the police even help if I did escape...or would they side with the kidnappers?

We finally arrived back at the sidewalk bank, and I filled out the Western Union money form once again. I put "$500" on the form and waited about five minutes (which seemed like twenty) for the return. During the waiting time, I tried keeping a congenial dialog going with the interpreter, feeling that she was still most likely my only ally. She was the only one with whom I could really communicate, and I had to keep that life-line open.

As the fax started printing, I stretched and strained to see if it said *declined* on it again…I couldn't tell. The teller was busy helping others at the other window and didn't immediately retrieve the form. Finally, he walked over and slid the paper out to me. It had been approved, but only in the amount of $450. Still, I was excited! Maybe this was the end of it, I thought.

Looking over my shoulder, the interpreter saw the total of the return and grew angry that the amount was not correct.

I said, "Listen, this is not your money anyway; you are stealing from me and you know it!"

Then the teller began counting the money out to me in forint as the interpreter had requested. At the time, the exchange rate was almost one hundred eighty to one, so the stack of money was about six to eight inches high. The interpreter demanded that I sit down on the bench, just three or four steps from the bank window, and count the money out to her. She said, "I'm the boss; I get the money!" This entire time I had thought the suit guy was in charge!

She motioned for the fifteen or so people to surround herself and me as I counted out the forint to her. *Finally, they will let me go*. At least, that's what I thought.

As I finished counting out the money, the interpreter said, "Now I want sixty more dollars!"

I couldn't believe what I was hearing. *Why sixty?* I thought. I argued with her and said, "I have given you guys eighty dollars in the restaurant, and now $450. That should be enough!"

She insisted, "We need sixty more dollars, now!"

I told her, "I will have to make *another* phone call to do that!" She readily agreed, so we headed back to the sidewalk phone once again.

With each trip to a phone, I knew it might actually be a trip away from the crowd so that they could dispose of me. My hope was that we weren't going back toward the river again. We started back down Váci Utca, fortunately, to the very first wall phone we had used.

When Becky answered the phone, I began speaking quietly because I didn't want the interpreter to hear my plans. "Becky, the group is asking for sixty more dollars, but I want to ask Western Union for one hundred more dollars." My plan was to keep the money this time and try to escape. I wanted to sound encouraging. "I will call you as soon as I am free, and I think this is probably the best opportunity for me to get away."

"Be careful!" she said.

"I will," I replied. "I will be okay."

Becky's Journal (A Different Perspective)

I didn't expect the agenda for this next phone call— they wanted more money! What? They wanted sixty more dollars, but Andy wanted me to send $100 so that he could make sure he had enough. We called Western Union again and got another control number. As I was telling Andy that the police were looking for him, the phone went dead! I dropped the phone lifelessly into my lap and looked at our pastor across the room. He told me later that my face went completely white at that point. I thought, *He's dead. His captors had to be listening in on the phone call and heard me tell him that the police were looking for him. They're going to kill him.* I was completely desperate. The people around me tried to console me…but it was just words to me. My head was ringing. The wait became long, and the crowd began to thin out, as evening was coming on in Borger and people needed to be with their own families.

I could still hear the sound of people in my home talking and making phone calls while Becky picked up another phone to dial Western Union. I knew this was probably my only chance to escape before my options ran out. She called once again, but this time she got the number fairly easily. I'm sure Michael had a clear understanding with Judith by now!

Becky came back on the phone and gave me the new control number, and then the kidnappers and I headed back to the bank.

CHAPTER 11

Escape

s we walked, I was planning to get the money in US dollars and then run into the Burger King across from the bank. From there, I could get to the subway. It was almost eleven o'clock, so I was worried that everything was about to shut down even though many people were still walking along Váci Utca. Burger King was my only option for escape—if it was closed, what would I do? Then it crossed my mind: *What time does the subway close?* During the two weeks that we had performed the drama, our latest ride on the subway had been at eleven at night, and if I remembered correctly, that was the last train into the central station. That particular train was from one of the outer sectors of Budapest, so my hope was that the Váci Utca station would be open a little later...I didn't really know. My other choice was a taxi. *Should I take a taxi? After all, one of these guys is a taxi driver!* Uncertainties aside, I felt it was now or never.

When I got to the bank again, I filled out the Western Union form for $100, as I had planned. After several minutes, the teller came back to give me the money, and I told him I wanted it in US currency.

The interpreter interrupted. *"No, forint!"*

I froze for a moment. That would interfere with my plan to take off with the money and use it to get home. I said, "No, US, because forint has too many bills to count!" Surprisingly, she allowed me to do this.

The teller gave me the money in twenties. Once again, the interpreter—or the boss, if she really was in charge—insisted that we sit on the bench to give her the money. I noticed that most of the group was now beginning to let their guard down a little and weren't as attentive to me as before. Some of the guys were flirting with a couple of girls who had just joined the group. I thought, *It's now or never!*

Just as we were sitting down to count out the money, I jumped up and forced my way through the kidnappers, knocking one girl to the ground. I ran into the Burger King about sixty feet away, dodging tourists and hearing many gasps and groans, and then planted myself at a table right in the middle of the restaurant. My heart was racing, and I desperately hoped that what I had just done would not exacerbate my situation.

With *everyone* in the restaurant and on the street watching, the suit guy came in and sat in the chair right in front of me. I put on my best John Wayne face and got tough. Trying to gain the attention of as many people as I could, I shouted to him, "No more; it's over!"

Then the strangest thing happened…he stood up and offered to shake my hand. I repeated, "It's over!"

He turned and joined his friends outside, glaring back at me through the window. They knew that I would eventually have to come out.

I had eaten in that Burger King many times before, and I knew there was only one way in and one way out, so I got up and walked toward the counter at the back. I positioned myself behind a column, out of view of the kidnappers outside, and asked, "Does anyone here speak English?"

One of the girls working behind the counter said, "I do."

To my left, I noticed a telephone on the wall just out of the line of sight of the kidnappers, who were still watching me. I told the girl, "I have been robbed, and I need you to call the police for me."

Showing concern, she picked up the phone, dialed the police, had a short conversation in Hungarian, and hung up. Then she told me, "You will need to go to the police station."

Just the thought of trying to leave made my heart beat even faster. "NO!" I insisted. "They need to come here!"

Seeming to understand, she called the police again and then told me that they were on their way. I knew I was *not* out of the woods yet; if it was the cop I had seen earlier, I was out of luck. I stayed by the phone, out of sight, waiting for the police to arrive.

Just minutes later, a small police car pulled up on the sidewalk, and the kidnappers scattered into the crowd. Two men and one lady officer entered the Burger King and were directed to me by everyone in the restaurant. I asked the employee to interpret as I quickly explained the entire story to the officers.

None of them spoke any English, but they walked me out to the police car, put me in the back with one of the officers, and began driving me around the area, pointing and asking questions in Hungarian. All I could figure was that they were trying to find out at which restaurant this had all started. I was thinking, *What if the police are in with these guys? They might take me back to the kidnappers.* Besides, I didn't know if I would even recognize the place at night.

They continued driving and occasionally pointing to places, but as far as I knew, we never passed it. Then, after about twenty minutes of driving around, they headed away from the Váci Utca area and started down dark, less-traveled streets.

I still felt unsafe, and now I really didn't have a clue where I was. Finally, we were driving down what seemed to be a one-way street, very narrow and dark, barely missing all the angled cars parked on either side of us. We slowed almost to a stop, and I noticed a small white sign swinging in the breeze with a single dim bulb lighting the word, "Policia." Seeing the police station began to make me feel a little better about the situation, but I still had my doubts.

I don't know why my confidence was still lacking; after all, it seemed that God had made that way of escape I was looking for. Yet I didn't feel free. I guess I can relate to the way many feel in their Christian walk: they have received Christ, but freedom still seems to elude them. God was about to solve this dilemma for me.

CHAPTER 12
THE AMBASSADOR

The police officers stopped the car and escorted me into the cold, dingy, echoing building, with several men smoking and loitering around. As I entered, I heard a man from behind a desk shout in his Hungarian brogue, "Robert Dietz?" I answered, "Igan!"

"Telefonia," he said. I took the phone from the desk officer and heard a gentleman with a clear American accent introduce himself as the US ambassador. "Mr. Dietz, I don't know who you are, but you must be important. I've had a dozen calls about you from senators and the FBI! Tell me what happened."

After I relayed the entire story to him, he expressed his concern and told me that he would come for me himself, but due to the embassy bombings, he could not. Then he told me that he was sending a taxi instead. The ambassador told me to wait in the office area until the driver came in to get me.

"Don't go outside!" he said. "Wait for the driver to come in for you! Let him call you by name; he will introduce himself as so-and-so, and he will escort you to the taxi."

The ambassador also gave me the taxi company name and car number to look for, and he told me that the driver would be dressed in all black. He apologized on behalf of the Hungarian people and said that he was sorry the incident had happened.

"Most of the Hungarian people are very kind and would be embarrassed to know that this happened to you, especially to an American."

I thanked him for his help and hung up.

I took a seat in the office area where most of the officers and detectives were gathered. They were all smoking heavily, as most Hungarians do, and were watching porn on the TV. I excused myself and waited in the front lobby alone. I watched out the window at the dark street, looking for car lights. It was hard to see very clearly because the room lights glared onto the window pane.

As I sat in the dingy lobby, I began to feel relief. I was not yet out of the woods, but speaking with the ambassador had brought a small amount of liberation. I continued looking for the taxi driver and couldn't help but have some doubt whether his assistance would be a safe avenue. I knew I might be walking right back into danger, but I didn't have any choice at this point.

After about five or ten minutes, the taxi finally arrived. I walked to the window and looked at the name and number of the taxi…it was a match.

The driver came inside the building dressed in all black and introduced himself to me with the correct name. He asked, "Are you Robert Dietz?"

"Yes, I am," I said.

We left the police station, and I looked around the dark area outside and in the backseat of the taxi before I got in to be sure no one was hidden there. All clear. After we got in the car, he told me that we needed to go get my things and change hotels. The ambassador hadn't mentioned changing hotels, so I wasn't sure what to do. I didn't have the money for a new hotel, and I couldn't assume it was paid for by the embassy. I told the driver to just take me to my hostel and I would be okay there. To be honest, I still wasn't sure that this taxi guy was legit; knowing that the first taxi driver had been involved with the kidnappers, I was still concerned that this one might take me back to the group.

We drove through mainly empty streets for about twenty minutes. I didn't recognize any landmarks or any familiar places at all. When we finally got to the hostel, it was after midnight, and I was just hoping to wake up from this crazy nightmare. We had to shake the outside chain-linked gate to stir the night watchman awake. The watchman finally made his way out to the gate to let us in. He kept asking if I was okay, and I said, "Yes."

The taxi driver told me he would be back at 5 a.m. to take me to the airport. He spoke to the watchman in Hungarian for several minutes and then left. I'm sure he was explaining what had happened to me and his plans to pick me up later that morning.

I got my key from the old man and started through the lobby to my room. I saw a pay phone on the lobby wall, so I made a phone call to Becky to let her know I was finally free. I heard her say, "He's free!" as the people in my house began to clap. I told her I was very tired, but I took the time to fill in most of the blanks with her. It was beginning to sink in—I was free. The story was over.

At least, I thought it was.

CHAPTER 13

JUST WHEN I THOUGHT
IT WAS OVER

Finishing the call with Becky and promising to call her again once I got to New York City, I headed to my room. I felt like I had just run a twenty-one-mile marathon…and finished last.

As I turned the corner and looked down the long hall toward my room, I noticed a full-length glass door at the end leading to the outside street. I had let down my guard; now I remembered, alarmingly, that the kidnappers had been to my room earlier. When I noticed the glass door, the adrenaline kicked in once again as I wondered if they might be watching me walk to my room. The hall was well lighted, so I wanted to rush down to my door and get out of sight as quickly as I could.

Then I began to wonder if someone might be in my room. As I put my key in the door and slowly opened it, I noticed all the lights were out and my windows were wide open. I took a quick survey of the room and then of the bathroom to my right to see if anyone was there. It seemed clear, so I shut and locked my room door behind me. Because the window was wide open, I closed the door quickly, hoping no one had seen me come in.

I dropped my backpack against the threshold to block light from coming in under the doorway and crawled across the room to the window. I lifted my head up slowly and looked outside to see if anyone was there.

A small black car was just fifteen feet away on the other side of the short rock wall which surrounded the back of the hostel. Inside the car were two men, who were smoking and occasionally glancing over at my window. There was only a small, dim streetlight about a half-block away on the other side of the men's car, and I didn't think they had spotted me coming in. With the poor lighting, I couldn't tell if I recognized them or not.

I crawled over and began carefully packing my larger backpack, just in case I needed to leave quickly. I packed everything except my toiletries, which were in the bathroom, and then attempted to slowly close the windows without alerting the men in the car. The windows were a vertical bi-fold type which latched at the bottom. From my knees, I reached up to the right vertical window and began moving it to the closed position, then the left window, and latched them both shut.

It took about five minutes to close each window. Slowly sliding the burlap curtains together took several minutes as well. I looked at my watch. It was about 1 a.m.

I decided to set my alarm to 4 a.m. in the unlikely event I fell asleep. Then I began occasionally looking out the window to see if the car was still there. It was about 2 a.m. when the car finally left the alley. I thought they might try to come in the hall door, or even get the old man to let them in, but after about fifteen minutes of quiet, I assumed they had left for good.

I fell down on my bed exhausted but couldn't sleep, partly because of adrenaline and partly because of the sticky, humid heat. I lay there for about an hour reliving the entire event and kicking myself for even allowing this to happen to me.

I should have just gone to Burger King to eat instead of an unknown restaurant. Going into the city to look for Amy's doll may have been a mistake. Not turning and leaving the restaurant at my first intuition of something wrong was stupid. I could be at the bottom of the Danube River right now!

These were just a few of the thoughts racing through my mind as I lay on my bed deprogramming. I was still not confident that I had totally escaped this ordeal, but I was able to thank the Lord for the temporary reprieve. I was hoping to *know* my fate soon.

Realizing that I wasn't going to sleep, I looked outside once again, then peeked under my door to be sure no one was in the hall. I slowly cracked the door open and looked down the hall both ways to confirm it was clear. It dawned on me that no one else was even in the hostel except the watchman, and he was completely on the other end of the building. There had been several drunken Russian tourists in the hostel during the week before, two floors above me, but now the place seemed empty.

At that point, I eased into the bathroom and took a quick shower by flashlight. The remainder of the time I spent looking out the window and watching the clock until it was time to meet the embassy driver at 5 a.m. That was the slowest three hours of my life. I really don't remember relaxing or feeling relief at this point at all, knowing that the only safety would come as I boarded the Swiss Air flight to Amsterdam in three hours.

Just before five, I searched the room with my flashlight to be sure I didn't leave anything behind. I cautiously opened the room door and walked down the hall to the lobby. I was really hoping the driver would be there so this could all finally end. I was so tired I couldn't have defended myself if the group was in the lobby waiting for me, a possibility which crossed my mind. I put on my best badge of courage and walked vigilantly down the hall, hoping for the best.

CHAPTER 14

A SURPRISE!

J ust as I walked through the lobby, the pay phone on which I'd called Becky started ringing. I thought *who would be calling at this time in the morning?* I wondered if it might be the taxi driver saying he couldn't come get me, or maybe the kidnappers after seeing me exit my room. Maybe the phone would wake the watchman so I wouldn't have to.

This was the only phone in the entire building, and it just kept ringing and ringing, so I decided to answer it. Chances were good it was someone for me.

The voice on the other end said, "Is this Andy?"

"Yes, who is this?" I asked.

The answer was a total surprise. "Troy!" the voice said. I knew Troy from my twin brother's youth group in Tulsa, Oklahoma. He had been in Budapest several summers performing the drama with other groups and acting as a team leader for Awe Star Ministries. Awe Star is Walker Moore's organization, and it actually owns the *Freedom* drama. Troy had also stayed at the same hostel while working with Awe Star.

After hearing about my kidnapping, he had just happened to remember the hostel number, so he decided to call in hopes of finding me there.

"News travels fast!" he said. Evidently a lot of people had heard about me being kidnapped. I told him I was just walking by the phone when he called and was on my way to the airport. The timing was amazing.

We talked for a few minutes, and I thanked him for calling

and told him everything was okay.

"I'm so glad you're safe!" he told me.

"Yeah, me too," I replied.

After I hung up, I cautiously walked through the lobby to the front door to see the same driver waiting there for me at the chain-linked gate. If he had not been there, my only option would have been to call another taxi, and that could have been a problem.

The phone call had not awakened the old man, so I reluctantly knocked on his window to wake him and give him my room key. He would need to unlock the gate and let me out anyway. After several knocks, the old man finally stirred; after all, it had been a long night for him as well. He sat on the side of his bed and slid on his shoes; then we walked out to the gate together. I shook his hand and got in the taxi.

We had about a thirty-minute ride to the airport, and as we turned into the terminal, we could see the sun just beginning to peek over the eastern horizon.

I had lived to see another sunrise.

CHAPTER 15

Now What?

The ambassador had thought through his care of me. The driver told me that he was to stay with me until my plane took off, which made me feel better.

As we ate breakfast and then walked around the airport, we both noticed a man dressed in a suit who seemed to be following us. We made several turns and loops just to see if he still followed, and he did. We decided to go to my gate and sit there until the plane boarded. The man sat in the gate area next to ours and read a newspaper until it was time to board. I noticed that he got in line about eight or ten people behind me. I boarded the plane and found an aisle seat near the front, and the man in the suit sat one row back and across the aisle from me.

I was very tired, so I slept off and on during the five-hour flight to Amsterdam, but because I thought I was being watched, the naps were short and not very sound.

Schiphol, in Amsterdam, was an airport I had traveled through many times, so I quickly exited the plane and got lost in the crowd and many shops, trying to lose the man in the suit. The secure area of Schiphol is similar to a three-story mall, so it is an easy place to lose someone. When I couldn't see any trace of him anymore, I went downstairs to the mall area to find a place to grab lunch and then headed to customs for the international flight to New York.

My bags were checked all the way from Budapest to JFK, so I went to the gate to get my boarding pass. I don't know how it happened, but the ticket agent said, "Sir, we will be boarding first class in just a few minutes." Somehow, I had been issued a first class ticket to New York. I just smiled and said thank you.

Knowing that I had a good seat, I waited near the ticket counter to board last and watched for the suit man. As far as I know, he never boarded the airplane, and I never saw him arrive in first class. I was able to get a little sleep between the occasional interruptions of regret, guilt, and relief from this twelve-hour nightmare.

I don't know that I have ever had that feeling before or since the kidnapping. It's hard to explain. My emotions moved from intense fear and urgency during the kidnapping to a mix between exhaustion and humiliation after I finally felt safe. It was as though the blood from my body had completely drained, and numbness and exhaustion had replaced it. My mind was racing from thoughts of how the events of the past twelve hours might have been avoided to visions of my body sinking to the bottom of the dirty, cold Danube River.

Nothing I had knowingly done was really responsible for my predicament, but guilt continued to attack me. *How did this happen to* me? *This kind of thing happens to others—not me!*

Becky's Journal [A Different Perspective]

It was hours before I heard from Andy again. His first words to me were, "I'm FREE!" I turned to my friends and repeated it, and there was instantaneous applause and cheering! We were all overcome with relief. I cried. It was overwhelming to know that Andy was in a safe place and his life had been spared. Of course, we were still worried because he was staying at the hostel and his captors knew where his room was. I knew I wouldn't be satisfied until I saw his feet planted on American soil!

After Andy's call, I called my children in Canyon, Texas, for the first time that day. I told them everything that had happened, and at first they thought I was joking. Even after I convinced them that it had really happened, they didn't understand the gravity of the situation. I'm not sure why I didn't call them while it was happening…I think I just wanted to spare them. I also knew it would be easy for me to transmit my fear.

Four hours later, Andy called me from the Budapest airport and had gone through customs, so we felt he was really safe. I didn't sleep at all that night— every scene of my day was rolling through my mind. My body would shake occasionally as I experienced that feeling of desperation all over again. My mind was consumed. I'd lived a very sheltered life growing up in the panhandle of Texas, and this was the stuff that happened in movies—not to ordinary people like me. It felt like I'd walked through a lifetime of experiences in a short eight hours.

The kids all came home on Saturday, and at 7:50 Saturday evening, we picked Andy up at the Amarillo airport. I'd never seen Andy so exhausted. And I'd never been so grateful.

New York was a welcome sight, and soon I transferred to the journey home. As the plane circled over the wheat fields of Amarillo and began its descent, I didn't know what to expect when I disembarked. I knew there would eventually be a lot of questions, but I honestly expected only my family to be there to pick me up.

I finally touched down in Amarillo to find a crowd of well-wishers, prayer warriors, and family members waiting for me. It was good to be home. To hug my wife and kids—something that just hours before, I hadn't known if I would do ever again. That was something I wouldn't take for granted anymore. It was good to see our friends and hug them as well, but I remember them staring at me as though in disbelief that I was actually there in flesh and blood.

A battle continued in my mind for weeks following my return home. Most people, but not all, were supportive of me. There were those who questioned my motives, my choice of restaurant, and my integrity. The thought of people raising those questions and doubts overwhelmed my thoughts for weeks afterward. Satan wants us to feel accused and guilty because he is the accuser! When he can't steal our salvation, he battles to steal our joy! I kept reminding myself who the real enemy was. It was not those who might have questions; the questions are legitimate. It was Satan, who "comes to steal, kill, and destroy" (John 10:10). I had to believe the truth and not people's assumptions. God was not surprised by the recent events. In fact, He had a purpose in all of it…and that was where my focus needed to be.

Not many people have their own personal FBI agent, but I was assigned an FBI agent who questioned me days later about the entire event. "Wilford Brimley," of *The Waltons* and *Cocoon* fame, would best describe my agent. He had the white felt Stetson cowboy hat and the long gray handlebar mustache. His voice even had the slow Texas drawl and rough, gravelly sound of Mr. Brimley. We made an appointment to meet at my house and have lunch. When he arrived at my door, he introduced himself and said, "Let's go grab a burger; I'm hungry!"

During lunch, I answered all of his questions and relayed

the entire story to him. The interview took place about a week after I returned home. I had already isolated myself a little from the experience, but to relive the story back to the agent sparked some of the doubts all over again.

When I finished, he said, "The FBI may never find out who was responsible for your kidnapping, but twenty years from now...who knows, we may have some answers for ya!"

It was during that meeting that I learned I'd been taken by the Hungarian Mafia. They were always looking for lone foreigners from whom they could extort money, and I don't think I was the first. He called me again, one year later, but that was the last I heard from the FBI.

After the FBI meeting, I was interviewed by two magazines and several newspapers, which really helped me to establish the facts in my mind. None of the publications got all the details correct, which was the motivation for me to write down the story myself.

I can honestly say that the kidnapping never did discourage me from my travels or wanting to minister in other countries. It only made me more determined to put precautions in place and to be better prepared. The previous year was supposed to have been the final project in Budapest anyway, had the president not requested a return. I would have traveled back to Budapest the next week had the opportunity presented itself, because I know it was an error on my part which had prompted the entire episode.

Beyond that, though, I knew that God had been in control. In fact, He had prepared the entire experience for me and taken care of me through it for a purpose of His own. And now that I was safe, it was time to identify that purpose—and learn to experience life.

CHAPTER 16

WHY?

The real question that continued to enter my mind during the ten-hour international flight to New York City was, *God, why did this happen to me? What are You trying to show me?* The answer came during the flight from DFW to Amarillo. It was almost as clear as a human voice speaking directly to me. God said, "Andy, as desperately as you desired to live…I want you to be that desperate to know Me!"

I felt a little like Joseph when his brothers sold him off out of jealousy. He had to wonder why…*but God* had a plan. My story is a "but God" story! Jesus was crucified, *but God!* Lazarus died, *but God!* Bartimaeus was blind, *but God!* I'm glad that even though we may be in what seems to be an insurmountable situation, God always has a plan, and He will speak to us! I was kidnapped and my life was threatened, *but God* intended to deliver me. More than that, He intended to bring me to a place of desperation for Him so that I could learn to live in a whole new way.

God had spoken to me in a similar way on two other occasions in my life that I remember. Once was during my college years when I had drifted so far from Him, and another time was twelve years later during a summer camp that I directed in Colorado. God never gives up, does He?

During my freshman year of college I was drawn away from the Lord, drifting in and out of fellowship with Him that year. I recall it being an intense battle—similar in intensity to being kidnapped, but in a very different way! In my college battle, my moral values were being tested. I was experimenting, or truthfully, testing God and my walk with Him. It finally came to the point where God made me choose. I knew God was battling for me, but I knew Satan was battling just as hard. This was not a drama…it was real. God brought me to a real and definite decision point. I knew it was a choice of life or death. I chose life! Had I made the wrong choice in college, my life could have been much different. I could have ended up a bum on the streets or even in prison.

The second life encounter with God was not a battle as before but rather a realization that I had unintentionally drifted from my walk with Him. This is where so many Christians are today; like a frog in the kettle, we feel the water slowly turned up to a boil before we're even aware of it. We don't just jump into boiling hot water…we slowly sink into passivity and apathy.

It was during a worship service at camp that God just moved on the entire group like I had never seen before. It wasn't worked up or contrived, but before we knew it, the entire group had fallen on their faces in repentance to God. People were not praying in groups, but everyone prayed individually. The prayer time lasted uninterrupted for seven hours. A gentle Colorado rain began to fall that night as if God was saying, "Welcome home!"

After the kidnapping, I knew this was not another one of those camp times. Sometimes God takes our face in His hands and gently reminds us to come back to Him, but this time, He needed to get my attention, to shake my world. I prefer gentle reminders, but they are not always what we need. Because of my brush with death, my complacency and dissatisfaction were challenged. I tried desperately to know Him with all my heart once again.

The biggest change that came from this experience was a constant awareness of God and His involvement in my life. I appreciated the life He gave me more fully, and I tried to take in every minute, every relationship, and every situation and see God in it. My worship was deeper, and my personal time with Him grew. I knew He had a perfect plan for me.

For several years after being kidnapped, my heart stayed desperately in tune with God. It was a wonderful experience, and I can say that God blessed my ministry and life in ways that could only be explained by Him. Then, as years passed, I allowed circumstances to begin to harden my heart again: church conflicts, community tragedies, busyness, and cynicism began to steal my joy.

Recently, God reminded me of a quote from one of my former pastors, Paul Burleson, a man who molded and developed more of my ministry than any other person. The quote is simple, and maybe not so profound, but very true: "What are you doing under the circumstances?"

We serve a God who holds the government upon His shoulders. At the name of Jesus, demons tremble. We serve a God who is the Name Above All Names, the King of Kings, the Lord of Lords, the Prince of Peace, the First, the Last, the Alpha, the Omega, the Almighty God! *What are we doing under the circumstances,* when we have a God who is over everything?

As I'm often reminded of my story, God continues to stir my heart to be desperate for Him. I can't let the daily circumstances of life distract me from the purpose and calling that God has for me. I need to be focused!

During my high school and college years, I ran the 120-yard high hurdles as one of my track events. It was always very easy to get distracted by the runners beside me as they would bump my hands or hit a hurdle. Many times I would even hear runners falling to the cinders and moaning as they hit the ground behind me. I could win only if I kept my sights on the finish line—not on the other struggling runners or even the next hurdle approaching, but on the finish line ahead.

During my junior year in high school, I won almost every race I entered, with the exception of the races my senior team-mate entered. He was always searching for that illusive 13.9 time. Very few hurdlers ever broke the 14.0 mark, but he was always close. I was usually just a step behind him, so I was antic-ipating my senior year when I would hopefully be able to win every race and break that 14.0 barrier myself.

My senior year came, but so did Randy Lightfoot (what a great name for a track star!). Randy was a skinny, tall freshman from the rival Plainview High School who was consistently run-ning 13.9 almost every meet. If I were to beat Randy, I would have to break the 14-second barrier.

One day during a track workout, in an attempt to improve my time, my coach, Jeep Webb, noticed that my feet were pointed slightly outward as I ran. His theory was that I should be able to trim my time if I just turned my feet inward as I ran and kept my focus on the finish line.

The very next meet brought Randy and me together in the finals for the district championship. As the gun fired, I began to pull slightly ahead of Randy and was ahead of him even over the last hurdle. The crowd and my teammates were all scream-ing and cheering. Then, I felt a knot in the back of my leg…I had pulled my hamstring. Yet, I was so focused that I was able to finish the final fifteen yards even with a pulled hamstring. I finished the race with a 13.9, but lost to Randy who ran a 13.6. Really, it was all about focus: focus on the finish line, and focus on my technique, which brought excellence even in a losing effort.

One Scripture that I've identified most with as a runner, and now as a runner in the Christian life, is Philippians 3:12–14: "Not that I have already obtained it or have already become perfect, but I press on so that I may lay hold of that for which also I was laid hold of by Christ Jesus. Brethren, I do not regard myself as having laid hold of it yet; but one thing I do: forgetting what lies behind and reaching forward to what lies ahead, I press on toward the goal for the prize of the upward call of God in Christ Jesus."

It is sometimes hard for us to keep our focus, but it is most important if we are to accomplish that which the Father has planned for each of us. This is where *the life* that I mentioned in the introduction comes in. We should always be seeking *truth* in our life, the truth that only God can give; otherwise we are just living life and not experiencing *the life* that God has planned for us. When we are desperate for God and living closely to Him, we will truly experience the way, the truth, and the life.

On one of our latest trips to Asia, our team was helping a farmer water his tobacco crop because the normally lush, vegetated region was experiencing an extended yearlong drought. The area had not had a single drop of rain for over six months during the traditional rainy season.

As our team was finishing the watering, using water bottles filled from a fifty-gallon barrel, God began speaking to me. He clearly told me to tell the farmer that our team wanted to pray with him for rain.

The people in this region of Asia had never met white people; not to mention they had never even heard the name of Jesus or anything about Him. So for me to pray with the farmer for rain was certainly a stretch! I began to reason with God that the farmer wouldn't understand, but God said, "Tell him you will pray for rain."

"God, what if it doesn't rain? We will look bad!" I argued.

Once again God said, "Tell him you want to pray to the one true God for rain!"

Reluctantly, I called the team together and told my interpreter that we were going to pray to the one true God for rain.

"What if it doesn't rain?" she said.

"I've already had this argument with God," I told her.

So we turned to the farmer and his wife, and I put my hand on his shoulder and told him that we wanted to pray to the one true God for rain. He agreed, and we prayed.

The farmer thanked us, and our team walked from the tobacco field to our "hotel" a mile away for the evening meal. The hotel had only four rooms, each sleeping six people in three double beds. The linens were seldom washed or changed, and there was no running water or electricity in the town. The only restroom was an open-air public "squatty potty" about a half-block away from the hotel. Many of the townspeople ate at the hotel restaurant, which was comprised of a covered patio and an open stove fueled by coal, with food washed and prepared on outside tables continually infested by hundreds of flies.

Our team moved to a lower patio after dinner to allow for others to come in and eat. I told the team that what we were about to do was risky, especially in a country where public worship was outlawed and pastors were regularly imprisoned and tortured for their faith. God instructed me to lead a worship and prayer meeting, asking Him to bring rain. I remind you that it had not rained in over six months, and there was not a cloud in the sky!

My youngest son led us in worship with a borrowed guitar, and we moved into the prayer time just after the sun had set over the western mountain behind me. The town was surrounded by mountains, and darkness came quickly.

During the final song of worship, I noticed four government officials enter and sit for supper at a table in the upper patio above us. One of the men sent the waitress down to our interpreter to ask what we were doing. I told the interpreter to tell them that we were praying to the one true God for rain. When the waitress returned with the answer, the group of men broke out in laughter.

We continued to pray, asking God to show Himself to these people who needed to know Him and His love so badly. After about forty-five minutes of intercession, asking God to move, I heard my wife's whisper telling me to look behind me over the mountain. To my surprise, I could see an intense lightning storm approaching. I stopped the prayer meeting for just a moment to show the team the lightning. Needless to say, our prayers intensified, and together as a group, we prayed believing that God would answer our prayers. At four o'clock that morning it began to rain, and it rained every day for several months thereafter.

I was afraid to listen to God on that day, fearing that I was wrong or that He would embarrass Himself. We need to learn to keep our spiritual radar up at all times, hear God, and obey what He says. This sensitivity to the Holy Spirit and His leading was what I had lost. I had slipped back into the rut of just going to church and indulging in a narcissistic "me world"! Before my kidnapping, life had become about me again: what I liked, what I wanted, what I needed, and not what God desired!

As I look around me, I fear that this is the state of today's church. For the most part, it has become about what we like, what we want, and what we need. If the church is not careful, we are in danger of becoming just like the older children of Israel, the first generation in the desert whom God gave up on— in fact, He destroyed them and began appealing to the younger generation, who moved into the Promised Land! If we do not regain our desperation for Him, we will become complainers, and disobedient, and selfish, and God will leave us to ourselves and move forward with a new and submissive generation.

I mentioned divine appointments at the beginning of this book. When a person is obedient to God, it seems that divine appointments just happen, and often when you least expect them. Eleven years after our last trip to Budapest, I was in my church office and received a phone call from a salesperson. We talked for a few minutes, and I noticed her unusual accent. I told her that she sounded Hungarian. She told me she had moved to the US from Budapest a year ago, and she wondered how I knew that she was Hungarian. I told her that we had taken drama teams to Budapest each summer for five years, and I had learned to recognize the accent.

Then she began to describe the drama to me. "I remember a sword fight and a crucifixion scene, and everyone wore masks," she said. "Is that your drama?"

I told her it was the drama we did, but there were some-times two or three teams in Budapest each summer. Then she told me that the team had given her a yellow *Four Spiritual Laws* booklet and had led her to the Lord. It was our team she had seen! We always carried *Four Spiritual Laws* with us each year.

Since being kidnapped, I have learned a lot of dos and don'ts that I've compiled into a missions training manual. I didn't let the experience stop me from traveling, but I did gain a lot of wisdom from it. Since the kidnapping, I have been to Mexico eighteen times; Brazil, the Philippines, and Israel once; and China thirty-three times.

At the Borger church, I have put in place many safeguards to protect against kidnapping, getting lost, and losing passports, and we have learned to recognize possible dangers. Procedures are even in place for natural disasters that can occur during mission projects. We add something new to the manual almost every trip…we never stop learning. Traveling in groups, especially "in country"; keeping leaders informed of team members' plans; the "watch your team member's back" rule; showing your partner your passport on both entering and departing an airplane; and keeping essentials in a fanny pack on your nightstand in case of an earthquake or some other unexpected event are a few of the changes that have been added to the manual as we've seen the need. Caution is always important. Any team needs to be over prepared. At the same time, there is a point at which we must trust God and not let fear keep us from the most important commission given to Christians. We must GO!

Not even the fear of death should keep us from doing God's will. If we continue to be desperate to hear God and follow His voice, His will is the best place we can be! Jeremiah 29:11–13 says, "'For I know the plans I have for you,' declares the Lord, 'plans for welfare and not for calamity to give you a future and a hope. Then you will call upon Me and come and pray to Me, and I will listen to you. You will seek Me and find Me when you search for Me with all your heart."

In my years of youth ministry, people would ask me after each camp experience why young people and adults have such awesome experiences there. Why it is that camp brings out such repentance and motivation to follow Christ?

My answer is that at camp we starve the flesh and feed the Spirit. At home we starve the Spirit and feed the flesh. Camp is a week away from television, computers, cell phones, and bad influences. It is a saturation of worship, Bible study, and good influences. This principle so influenced me at camp one year that my wife and I decided to take the television out of our house. Yes! Our four kids were upset at first, but we began to notice the family coming together just to talk. Talking became our entertainment. Now, when our grown kids come home for the holidays, we all still gather in the living room and just talk. Even the grandkids join us from time to time just to listen.

To be desperate for God means to desire the things of God more than the things of this world. Starve the flesh and feed the Spirit. I remember hearing a story from a preacher several years ago that illustrates my point well. A young man was nearing the end of his internship with a well-known Bible scholar. Every day, the intern and the elderly scholar would walk through the woods near the old man's home and discuss various topics.

Their walk would take them through the woods and over a small creek and back. The young intern had the same question every day for the old man, but he never did answer it. The question he would ask was, "How can I know God?"

One day while crossing the creek on their daily walk, the young man asked the question once again: "How can I know God?" Without warning, the old man grabbed the young man by the back of his neck and drove his face into the water of the frigid creek. The young man began to struggle to free himself from the grip of the old man but couldn't. Finally, when the young man couldn't hold his breath any longer, the old man pulled his face out of the water and released his grip.

"What are you doing?" the young man shouted.

"When you desire God as much as you desired your next breath...then you will know God!" the old man replied.

On the airplane from New York that day, God told me, "As desperate as you were to live, be that desperate to know Me." God is not calling us to remove ourselves from the world, but rather for our transformed lives to be an inspiration to the world. As God's priests and ambassadors, we are to represent God wherever we are. "Therefore be imitators of God, as beloved children; and walk in love, just as Christ also loved you and gave Himself up for us, an offering and a sacrifice to God as a fragrant aroma" (Ephesians 5:1–2).

That's experiencing life! It is not just living it or getting through it, but it is representing God! When we do this, life takes on an entirely different dimension. Seldom has a week passed now that I don't see God doing things with me that can only be explained by Him. I pray, "Lord, let me never again slip into passivity, apathy, and indifference, but keep my heart desperate to know You and the power of Your resurrection!"

Oh yes! For those of you who remember what started this entire story, my daughter never did get her doll…but she did get her dad back!

ABOUT THE AUTHOR

~≋~

A ndy Dietz was Texas born and raised with his twin brother, Phil, and older brother, Mike. At eight years old, he and his twin began singing in harmony for small church gatherings, eventually performing in major coliseums around the world. During high school, Andy was selected to the All-Area Choirs, as well as first chair All-State Choir in his senior year. He also played football and ran one of the nation's best times in the 120-yard high hurdles in track. While still teenagers, Andy and Phil began a singing ministry, traveling and performing as The Dietz Brothers.

Andy attended West Texas A&M University on a full music scholarship, graduating with a bachelor's degree in mass communications and a double minor in music and English. During their junior year, Andy and Phil joined the gospel quartet, The Royalheirs. They recorded four albums with the Royalheirs and toured with other gospel quartets, including the Stamps Quartet. After college graduation, Andy and his brother were selected to tour as part of a college ensemble with the USO to military bases throughout the Caribbean. Following the USO tour, they traveled again as The Dietz Brothers and were featured artists in Texas, Oklahoma, Missouri, and Florida Youth Evangelism Conferences.

In 1981, Andy began student ministry at Second Baptist Church, Amarillo, Texas. Next he moved to Broken Arrow, Oklahoma, where he grew the student ministry at First Baptist Church from four hundred to over six hundred. While there, Andy was asked to help develop their small, struggling student choir; in just six months, it grew to nearly three hundred voices.

Desiring to raise his family in a smaller city, Andy accepted a student ministry position in Borger, Texas. The ministry blossomed to several hundred students, with missions playing a vital part, prompted by Andy's orphanage ministry during his days with The Dietz Brothers.

The Borger church developed a tremendous heart for missions, and Andy was invited to become the pastor of missions and evangelism. Since then, he has led thirty-three medical mission teams to China, eighteen teams to Mexico, and five to Budapest, Hungary. He has also led and organized trips to Switzerland, Brazil, Russia, Poland, and the Philippines. Over three hundred individual church members from Borger have traveled on foreign mission trips with Andy, and the church has sent out thirteen missionaries from their fellowship.

Andy also served on the missions board for the Southern Baptists of Texas.

He is currently the pastor of First Baptist Church in Groom, Texas. In addition to writing a memoir about his Mafia kidnapping in Budapest, Andy's recent writing addresses topics such as student ministry, missions training, and truth. He and his wife, Becky, have four children, who are all involved in ministry, and ten amazing grandchildren.

Visit andydietz.net.

A joyful, brown-eyed, Mexican orphan named Jacabo helped inspire me to follow the call to missions.

The elegant Budapest skyline.

Stopping for a quick pose in the airport with our 1998 drama team from Borger, Texas. I'm in the back row, third from the left.

Our team performing as the Evil Knights in a scene from the drama *Freedom*.

While performing in "Prostitute Park," our team faced persecution, followed by a remarkable display of the transformative power of Christ!

After our drama performance, Hungarian gang members (shown here) received Christ.

Following the successful drama tour, I traveled from Budapest to Moscow to deliver support funds from our church in Borger to a Russian church.

While in Russia, I stayed in the home of James, a former student from Borger now ministering in Moscow.

The Budapest night market.

Vaci Utca Street, in Budapest. After my side trip to Russia, I returned to this popular shopping area to purchase a birthday gift for Amy. On the left side of the street is the bank where some of my kidnapping nightmare played out. On the right is the Burger King where I finally made my escape.